*Advent Reflections
from Church History*

Advent Reflections
from Church History

EDITED & INTRODUCED BY
Ron Prosise & Ryan Rippee

Heritage Seminary Press, Cambridge, Ontario, Canada
An imprint of H&E Publishing, West Lorne, Ontario, Canada

heritageseminarypress.com

© 2025 Ron Prosise and Ryan Rippee. All rights reserved. This book may not be reproduced, in whole or in part, without written permission from the publishers.

Unless otherwise indicated, Scripture quotations are from the ESV® Bible (The Holy Bible, English Standard Version®), © 2001 by Crossway, a publishing ministry of Good News Publishers. Used by permission. All rights reserved.

Cover & book design: Janice Van Eck

Advent Reflections from Church History
Edited and Introduced by Ron Prosise and Ryan Rippee

ISBN 978-1-77484-190-7 (paperback)
ISBN 978-1-77484-191-4 (eBook)

Contents

Foreword *by Michael A.G. Azad Haykin* — vii
Introduction — ix

Day 1	Tertullian	1
Day 2	Athanasius	5
Day 3	Basil of Caesarea	9
Day 4	John Chrysostom	13
Day 5	Augustine	17
Day 6	John Wycliffe	21
Day 7	Martin Luther	25
Day 8	John Calvin	29
Day 9	Catherine Parr	33
Day 10	Richard Sibbes	37
Day 11	Jeremiah Burroughs	41
Day 12	Isaac Ambrose	45
Day 13	John Flavel	49
Day 14	Catharina Regina von Greiffenberg	53
Day 15	Isaac Watts	57
Day 16	John Wesley	61
Day 17	Jonathan Edwards	65
Day 18	George Whitefield	69
Day 19	John Newton	73
Day 20	Hannah More	77
Day 21	J.C. Ryle	81
Day 22	Charles Haddon Spurgeon	85
Day 23	Dwight L. Moody	89
Day 24	G. Campbell Morgan	93
Day 25	D. Martyn Lloyd-Jones	97
Day 26	Dietrich Bonhoeffer	101
Day 27	J.I. Packer	105
Day 28	James Montgomery Boice	109

Foreword

Christians, of all people, ought to be givers of thanks. We have so much to be grateful for, not the least of which is being the heirs of a rich tradition of Christian wisdom. To recall the words and lives of our Christian forebears is an act of deep gratitude. Since many of us, though, do not have the time or resources to study in detail the writings of our predecessors in the faith, a compilation like this one is so vital.

What binds this particular volume together is the Christian celebration called *Advent*, the beginning of the church year, in which we who are believers in the Lord Jesus remember his advents: the first as a babe in the manger, a necessary step in his incarnation and on the road to the cross; the second as the Lord of glory from heaven in triumph over all of the forces of evil.

More and more of us are recognizing the wisdom of drawing upon the Christian year that is organized around the key events of salvation history. Advent prepares us for the celebration of *the* momentous turning-point of all of history, namely, the incarnation.

May this small collection of wise reflections from past saints help to prepare all who read this work to celebrate the real meaning of Christmas and live in the light of the glory of the incarnate Christ.

Michael A.G. Azad Haykin
Dundas, Ontario
In the year of our Lord 2025, October 17.

Introduction

The word *advent* is from the Latin *Adventus*, which means coming. Historians believe that Advent began first as a preparation for the baptism of new Christians at the January feast of Epiphany, which was the celebration of Christ's incarnation represented by the visit of the Magi to the baby Jesus (Matthew 2:1–11). By the sixth century, the emphasis shifted to the coming of Christ. But this celebration was not of Jesus' first coming as Saviour, but his second as Judge. Advent season was not explicitly connected to Christ's first coming until the Middle Ages. It then incorporated both aspects of Jesus' coming, past and future. Today the Advent season is observed as a preparation for Christmas, a reflection on the grace of God in Christ, as well as the promise of the Lord's coming again.

Protestant Christians observe Advent beginning on the fourth Sunday before Christmas and ending on Christmas Eve, December 24. And so, depending on the year, the Advent season is from 22 to 28 days in length.

As the Christmas season is typically a busy one, countless believers have found that Advent devotionals are a wonderful way to fix their eyes on Jesus during this special time. There are many such wonderful advent devotionals in print. We saw the opportunity to glean from the writings of faithful men and women from ages past to compile *Advent Reflections from Church History*, reading their wise insights and passionate love for Jesus Christ as we consider the mystery, wonder and grace of our Saviour, *Immanuel*, God with us.

Ron Prosise and Ryan Rippee, editors

Day 1

Tertullian
(c. 155-c. 220)

Tertullian was an elder and theologian in the church at Carthage, writing a number of books defending the Christian faith. He is known for coining the term *Trinitas* or *Trinity* in English to defend monotheism alongside the full deity of our Lord Jesus as well as the Holy Spirit.

∞∞∞∞∞∞∞∞∞∞∞∞∞∞∞∞∞∞∞

And behold, you will conceive in your womb and bear a son, and you shall call his name Jesus (Luke 1:31).

Touching then the discussion of his flesh, and of his nativity, and incidentally of his name *Immanuel*, let this suffice. For *Christ* means *anointed*, and to be anointed is certainly an affair of the body. He who had not a body, could not by any possibility have been anointed; he who could not by any possibility have been anointed, could not in any wise have been called Christ. It is a different thing, if he only assumed the phantom of a name too. But how was he to insinuate himself into being believed by the Jews, except through a name which was usual and familiar among them? Then it is a fickle and deceptive God whom you describe!

Now if he caught at the name *Christ*, why did he wish to be called *Jesus* too, by a name which was not so much looked for by the Jews? When Hoshea the son of Nun (Numbers 13:8) was destined to be the successor of Moses, is not his old name then changed, and for the first time he is called *Joshua* (Numbers 27:18)? It is true, you say. This, then, we first observe, was a figure of him who was to come. For inasmuch as Jesus Christ was to introduce a new generation (because we are born in the wilderness of this world) into the promised land which flows with milk and honey, that is, into the possession of eternal life, than which nothing can be sweeter; inasmuch, too, as this was to be brought about not by Moses, that is to say, not by the discipline of the law, but by Joshua, by the grace of the gospel, our circumcision being effected by a knife of stone, that is, (by the circumcision) of Christ, for Christ is a rock (or stone; 1 Corinthians 10:4), therefore that great man, who was ordained as a type of this mystery, was actually consecrated with the figure of the Lord's own name, being called *Joshua*. This name Christ himself even then testified to be his own, when he talked with Moses. For who was it that talked with him, but the Spirit of the Creator, which is Christ? When he therefore spoke this commandment to the people, "Behold, I send an angel before you to guard you on the way and to bring you to the place that I have prepared. Pay careful attention to him and obey his voice; do not rebel against him, for he will not pardon your transgression, for my name is in him" (Exodus 23:20–21). He called him an angel indeed, because of the greatness of the powers which he was to exercise, and because of his prophetic office, while announcing the will of God; but Joshua also (Jesus), because it was a type of his own future name. Often did he confirm that name of his which he had thus conferred upon (his servant); because it was not the name of angel, nor Hoshea, but Joshua (Jesus), which he had commanded him to bear as his usual appellation for the time to come. Since, therefore, both these names are suitable to the Christ of the Creator, they are proportionately unsuitable to the non-Creator's Christ; and so indeed is all the rest of (our Christ's) destined course. In short, there must now for the future be made between us that certain and equitable rule, necessary to both sides, which shall determine that there ought to be absolutely nothing at all in common between the Christ of the other god and the Creator's Christ. For you will have as great a necessity to maintain their diversity as we have to resist it, inasmuch as you will be as unable to show that the Christ of the other god has come, until you have proved him to be a far different being from the Creator's Christ, as we, to claim him (who has come) as the Creator's, until we have shown him to be such a one as the Creator has appointed. Now respecting their names, such is our conclusion against (Marcion) I claim for myself Christ; I maintain for myself Jesus.[1]

An encouragement to prayer by Tertullian

It begins with witness to God and the reward of faith, when we say: "Father, who art in heaven" [Matthew 6:9]. For we are both praying to God and setting forth our faith, the reward of which is the right to call him by this name. It is written to them that have believed in him, he hath given the power to be called sons of God."[2]

---

[1] *Tertullianus Against Marcion*, ed. Alexander Roberts and James Donaldson (Edinburgh: T. & T. Clark, 1868), 148–152.
[2] *Tertullian's Treatises: Concerning Prayer, Concerning Baptism*, trans. Alexander Souter (London: The MacMillan Company, 1919), 21.

Day 2

Athanasius
(c. 296-373)

Athanasius was the pastor of the church in Alexandria, Egypt. He was exiled from his pastorate five times for defending the full deity of Jesus Christ. His most famous book is *On the Incarnation*. He was also at the Council of Nicaea and instrumental in the formulation of the Nicene Creed.

But we see him who for a little while was made lower than the angels, namely Jesus (Hebrews 2:9).

The Word, perceiving that in no other way could the corruption of men be undone save by death as a necessary condition, while it was impossible for the Word to suffer death, being immortal, and Son of the Father; to this end he takes to himself a body capable of death, that it, by partaking of the Word who is above all, might be worthy to die in the stead of all, and might, because of the Word which was come to dwell in it, remain incorruptible, and that thereafter corruption might be stayed from all by the grace of the resurrection. And like as when a great king has entered into some large city and taken up his abode in one of the houses there, such city is at all events held worthy of high honour, nor does any enemy or bandit any longer descend upon it and subject it; but on the contrary, it is thought entitled to all care, because of the king's having taken up his residence in a single house there: so, too, has it been with the Monarch of all. For now that he has come to our realm, and taken up his abode in one body among his peers, henceforth the whole conspiracy of the enemy against mankind is checked, and the corruption of death which before was prevailing against them is done away. For the race of men had gone to ruin, had not the Lord and Saviour of all, the Son of God, come among us to meet the end of death.

Now in truth this great work was peculiarly suited to God's goodness. For if a king, having founded a house or city, if it be beset by bandits from the carelessness of its inmates, does not by any means neglect it, but avenges and reclaims it as his own work, having regard not to the carelessness of the inhabitants, but to what he himself seems fit; much more did God the Word of the all-good Father not neglect the race of men, his work, going to corruption: but, while he blotted out the death which had ensued by the offering of his own body, he corrected their neglect by his own teaching, restoring all that was man's by his own power. And of this one may be assured at the hands of the Saviour's own inspired writers, if one happen upon their writings, where they say: "For the love of Christ controls us, because we have concluded this: that one has died for all, therefore all have died; and he died for all, that those who live might no longer live for themselves but for him who for their sake died and was raised" (2 Corinthians 5:14–15). And again: "But we see him who for a little while was made lower than the angels, namely Jesus, crowned with glory and honor because of the suffering of death, so that by the grace of God he might taste death for everyone" (Hebrews 2:9). Then he also points out the reason why it was necessary for none other than God the Word himself to become incarnate; as follows: "For it was fitting that he, for whom and by whom all things exist, in bringing many sons to glory, should make the founder of their salvation perfect through suffering" (Hebrews 2:10), by which words he means, that it belonged to none other to bring man back from the corruption which had begun, than the Word of God, who had also made them from the beginning.

And that it was in order to the sacrifice for bodies such as his own that the Word himself also assumed a body, to this, also, they refer in these words: "Since therefore the children share in flesh and blood, he himself likewise partook of the same things, that through death he might destroy the one who has the power of death, that is, the devil, and deliver all those who through fear of death were subject to lifelong slavery" (Hebrews 2:14–15).[1]

Prayer of Athanasius

I will never cease to bless thee, O thou who endures forever. Thou art Jesus, the Son of the Father. Yea, Amen. Thou art he who commandeth the cherubim and the seraphim. Yea, Amen. Thou hast existed with the Father, in truth always. Yea, Amen. Thou rulest the angels. Yea, Amen. Thou art the power of the heavens. Yea, Amen. Thou art the crown of the martyrs. Yea, Amen. Thou art the deep counsel of the saints. Yea, Amen. Thou art he in whom the deep counsel of the Father is hidden. Yea, Amen. Thou art the mouth of the prophets. Yea, Amen. Thou art the tongue of the angels. Yea, Amen. Thou art Jesus my life. Yea, Amen.[2]

---

[1] *St. Athanasius on the Incarnation*, trans. Archibald Robinson (London: D. Nutt, 1891), 16–18.
[2] *Miscellaneous Coptic Texts in the Dialect of Upper Egypt*, ed. E.A. Wallis Budge (London: The British Museum, 1915), 1017–1018.

Day 3

Basil of Caesarea
(330-379)

Pastor of Caesarea in Cappadocia, Basil was a defender of the full deity of our Lord Jesus Christ in his work *Against Eunomius*. He was also instrumental in defending the full deity of the Holy Spirit in his work *On the Holy Spirit*.

Beloved, do not believe every spirit, but test the spirits to see whether they are from God, for many false prophets have gone out into the world. By this you know the Spirit of God: every spirit that confesses that Jesus Christ has come in the flesh is from God, and every spirit that does not confess Jesus is not from God (1 John 4:1-3).

I have received the letter which you, right honorable brothers, have sent me concerning the circumstances in which you are placed. I thank the Lord that you have let me share in the anxiety you feel as to your attention to things needful and deserving of serious heed. But I was distressed to hear that over and above the disturbance brought on the churches by the Arians, and the confusion caused by them in the definition of the faith, there has appeared among you yet another innovation, throwing the brotherhood into great dejection, because, as you have informed me, certain persons are uttering, in the hearing of the faithful, novel and unfamiliar doctrines which they allege to be deduced from the teaching of Scripture. You write that there are men among you who are trying to destroy the saving incarnation of our Lord Jesus Christ, and, so far as they can, are overthrowing the grace of the great mystery unrevealed from everlasting, but manifested in his own times, when the Lord, when he had gone through all things pertaining to the cure of the human race, bestowed on all of us the benefit of his own sojourn among us. He was himself manifested in the flesh, "born of woman, born under the law, to redeem those who were under the law, so that we might receive adoption as sons (Galatians 4:4–5).

If, then, the sojourn of the Lord in flesh has never taken place, the Redeemer paid not the fine to death on our behalf, nor through himself destroyed death's reign. For if what was reigned over by death was not that which was assumed by the Lord, death would not have ceased working his own ends, nor would the sufferings of the God-bearing flesh have been made our gain; he would not have killed sin in the flesh; we who had died in Adam should not have been made alive in Christ; the fallen to pieces would not have been framed again, the shattered would not have been set up again; that which by the serpent's trick had been estranged from God would never have been made once more his own. All these benefits are undone by those that assert that it was with a heavenly body that the Lord came among us. And if the God-bearing flesh was not ordained to be assumed of the lump of Adam, what need was there of the holy virgin? But who has the audacity now once again to renew by the help of sophistical arguments and, of course, by scriptural evidence, that old dogma now long ago silenced? For this impious doctrine of the seeming is no novelty. It was started long ago by the feeble-minded Valentinus, who, after tearing off a few of the apostle's statements, constructed for himself this impious fabrication, asserting that the Lord assumed the "form of a servant," and not the servant himself, and that he was made in the "likeness," but that actual manhood was not assumed by him. Similar sentiments are expressed by these men who can only be pitied for bringing new troubles upon you.

These, brothers, are the mysteries of the church; these are the traditions of the Fathers. Every man who fears the Lord, and is awaiting God's judgement, I charge not to be carried away by various doctrines. If anyone teaches a different doctrine and refuses to agree to the sound words of the faith, rejecting the oracles of the Spirit, and making his own teaching of more authority than the lessons of the Gospels, of such an one beware. May the Lord grant that one day we may meet, so that all that my argument has let slip I may supply when we stand face to face! I have written little when there was much to say, for I did not like to go beyond my letter's bounds. At the same time, I do not doubt that to all that fear the Lord a brief reminder is enough.[1]

Prayer of Basil

The One who is, Master, Lord, God, Father almighty, truly worthy, just, and fitting for magnificent praise; of your holiness, we praise you, we sing to you, we glorify you, we worship you, we give thanks to you, we glorify the only true God, and we offer to you, with a contrite heart and a spirit of humility, this rational worship of ours, because you have granted us the knowledge of your truth. And who is worthy to speak of your power, to make known all your praises, or to narrate all your wonders at all times? Master of all, Lord of heaven and earth, of all creation visible and invisible, who sits on the throne of glory, and looks upon the depths, unbeginning, unseen, incomprehensible, unchangeable, the Father of our Lord Jesus Christ, the great God and Saviour of our hope, who is the image of your incomprehensibility, the seal equal in essence, revealing yourself as the Father, Living Word, true God, pre-eternal wisdom, life,

---

[1] *A Select Library of Nicene and Post-Nicene Fathers of the Christian Church*: Vol. VIII, ed. Philip Schaff and Henry Wace (New York: The Christian Literature Company, 1895), 300–301.

sanctification, power, the true light from which the Holy Spirit proceeds, the Spirit of truth, the grace of adoption, the first fruits of the inheritance to come, the beginning of eternal goods, the life-giving power, the source of sanctification, before whom all creation, both rational and intellectual, bows down, and to whom it sends up unceasing doxologies, for all things are yours.[2]

---

[2] *The Liturgies of S. Mark, S. James, S. Clement, S. Chrysostom, S. Basil*, ed. John Mason Neale (London: Richard Dickinson, 1896), 156.

Day 4

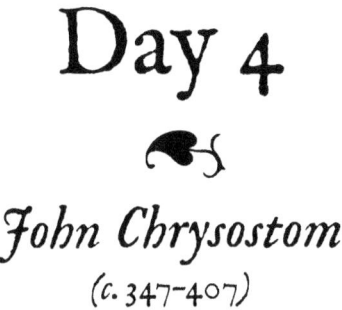

John Chrysostom
(c. 347-407)

Chrysostom was given the nickname "Golden-mouth" for his eloquent preaching. He was a pastor in Antioch, and later served as Archbishop of Constantinople. He is known as being one of the greatest expositors of the early church.

For the law was given through Moses; grace and truth came through Jesus Christ. No one has ever seen God; God the only Son, who is at the Father's side, he has made him known (John 1:17-18).

From what sort of thought sequence did John arrive at this statement? Having shown the great superiority of the gifts of Christ and that there is an infinite difference between them and those dispensed through Moses, he wished to conclude by mentioning the probable cause of the difference. As Moses was a servant, he was the dispenser of more lowly things; but as Christ was Master and King and Son of a King, he provided much greater things for us, since he is always with the Father and continually beholds him. For this reason, also, John went on to say, "No one has ever seen God."

What, then, shall we say to Isaiah, who affirmed: "I saw the Lord sitting upon a throne, high and lifted up" (Isaiah 6:1)? Moreover, what shall we say to John himself, who testified, "Isaiah said these things because he saw his glory" (John 12:41)? And what to Ezekiel? For he, also, saw him resting on the cherubim (Ezekiel 10:1). And what to Daniel? For he likewise declared, "The Ancient of Days took his seat" (Daniel 7:9). And what to Moses himself, who said, "Please show me your glory" (Exodus 33:18)? Jacob also received his name because of this privilege when he was called Israel, for Israel means "one who sees God." Indeed, others also have beheld him. How is it, then, that John said, "No one has ever seen God"? He was affirming that all those instances were manifestations of his condescension, not the vision of pure Being itself. If they had actually seen the very nature of God, they would not have beheld it under different appearances. For, that which is itself simple, and without shape, and not made up of parts, and not restricted by limits, does not sit nor stand nor walk about, since all these are functions of material bodies.

However, what God actually is, not only have the prophets not seen, but not even angels or archangels. If you ask them, you will not hear them reply anything about his substance, but only singing, "Glory to God in the highest, and on earth peace among those with whom he is pleased!" (Luke 2:14). If you desire to learn something even from the cherubim or seraphim, you will hear the mystical melody of his holiness and that "heaven and earth are full of his glory" (Isaiah 6:1–3). If you inquire of the higher powers, you will discover nothing else than that their one work is to praise God, for, "Praise him, all his hosts" the psalmist said (Psalm 148:2).

Therefore, the Son alone sees him, and also the Holy Spirit. How, in truth, could created nature see the Uncreated? Indeed, if we cannot even succeed in seeing clearly any immaterial power whatsoever, even though it is created—and this often has been illustrated in the case of the angels—much less can we attain to the vision of the immaterial and uncreated Being. For this reason, Paul, also, said, "whom no one has ever seen or can see" (1 Timothy 6:16).

Does this prerogative, then, belong to the Father only, and not also to the Son? Perish the thought! Certainly it also belongs to the Son. And to show that it does also belong to him, listen to Paul making this point clear in the words, "He is the image of the invisible God" (Colossians 1:15). Now, since he is the image of the invisible, he himself also is invisible, since otherwise he could not be that image.

Therefore, since we have been deemed worthy of a greater and more perfect teaching, no longer through prophets, but through the Son of God preaching to us in these latter days, let us give evidence of a much better life and one more worthy of the honour. It would be strange if, while he condescends to such an extent that he no longer wills to speak to us through servants, but through himself, we show no greater effects of this than our predecessors. To be sure, they had Moses as instructor, but we have the Lord of Moses. May it be that we all may attain to this by the grace and mercy of our Lord Jesus Christ, through whom and with whom glory be to the Father, together with the Holy Spirit, now and always, and forever and ever. Amen.[1]

Prayer of John Chrysostom

Worthy and righteous are you to be praised, to be extolled, to be glorified, to be thanked, to be worshipped in every place of your dominion. For you are God incomprehensible, boundless, unsearchable, inexhaustible, and being, as you are, eternally the same, you are the only begotten Son, and your Holy Spirit, even before time began, brought us into being from non-being, and when we fell, you raised us up again, and in all things you accomplish everything, even leading us to heaven, to the kingdom you have graciously promised us.[2]

---

[1] Saint John Chrysostom, *The Fathers of the Church*, trans. Sister Thomas Aquinas Goggin (New York: Cima Publishing Company, 1947), 142–150.
[2] *The Liturgies of S. Mark, S. James, S. Clement, S. Chrysostom, S. Basil*, ed. John Mason Neale (London: Richard Dickinson, 1896), 132.

Day 5

Augustine
(354-430)

Augustine was the pastor in the city of Hippo Regius in North Africa. He is known for his many books, particularly his *Confessions, On the Trinity* and *The City of God*. He is considered the greatest Latin-speaking theologian of the early church.

◇◇◇◇◇◇◇◇◇◇◇◇◇◇◇◇◇◇◇◇◇◇◇◇◇◇

Faithfulness springs up from the ground (Psalm 85:11).

The birthday of our Lord and Saviour, Jesus Christ, on which "Truth springs from the earth" and the procession of day from day extending even unto our time began, has, with the return of its anniversary, dawned upon us today as deserving of special celebration. "Let us rejoice and be glad" [Psalm 118:24] for the faith of Christians holds fast to the joy which the lowliness of such sublimity has offered to us.

Exult, you who are just; it is the birthday of the Justifier. Exult, you who are weak and ill; it is the birthday of the Saviour. Exult, you who are captives; it is the birthday of the Redeemer. Exult, you who are slaves; it is the birthday of the Ruler. Exult, you who are free; it is the birthday of the Liberator. Exult, all Christians; it is the birthday of Christ.

He who sustains the world lay in a manger, a wordless Child, yet the Word of God. Him whom the heavens do not contain the bosom of one woman bore. She ruled our King; she carried him in whom we exist; she fed our Bread. O manifest weakness and marvelous humility in which all divinity lay hid! By his power he ruled the mother to whom his infancy was subject, and he nourished with truth her whose breasts suckled him. May he who did not despise our lowly beginnings perfect his work in us, and may he who wished on account of us to become the Son of Man make us the sons of God.

Let us joyfully celebrate the coming of our salvation and redemption. Let us celebrate the festal day on which the great and timeless One came from the great and timeless day to this brief span of our day. He "became to us wisdom from God, righteousness and sanctification and redemption, so that, as it is written, 'Let the one who boasts, boast in the Lord'" [1 Corinthians 1:30–31].

When the psalmist had said: "Truth is sprung out of the earth," he quickly added: "and justice has looked down from heaven." He did this lest mortal frailty, presumptuously appropriating this justice to itself, should call these blessings its own, and lest man should reject the justice of God in his belief that he is justified, that is, made just through his own efforts. "Truth is sprung out of the earth" because Christ who said: "I am the truth" [John 14:6] was born of a virgin; and "justice has looked down from heaven" because, by believing in him who was so born, man has been justified not by his own efforts but by God. "Truth is sprung out of the earth" because "the Word became flesh," and "justice has looked down from heaven" because "every good and perfect gift is from above" [James 1:17]. "Truth is sprung out of the earth," that is, his flesh was taken from Mary; and "justice has looked down from heaven" because "no one can receive anything unless it is given to him from heaven" [John 3:27].

"Having been justified therefore by faith, let us have peace with God through our Lord Jesus Christ, through whom we also have access by faith into this grace in which we stand and we rejoice in the hope of the glory of God" [Romans 5:1–2]. With these few words, which you recognize as those of the apostle, it gives me pleasure, my brothers, to mingle a few passages of the psalm and to find that they agree in sentiment. "Having been justified by faith, let us have peace with God" because "justice and peace have kissed" [Psalm 85:10]; "through our Lord Jesus Christ" because "truth is sprung out of the earth"; "through whom we also have access by faith unto this grace in which we stand, and we rejoice in the hope of the glory of God." Let us rejoice, then, in this grace so that our glory may be the testimony of our conscience [2 Corinthians 1:12] wherein we glory not in ourselves but in the Lord. Hence the psalmist, in speaking of the Lord, has said: "My glory and the lifter up of my head" [Psalm 3:3]. Examine it as a benefit, as an inducement, as a token of justice, and see whether you find anything but a gracious gift of God.[1]

Prayer of Augustine

Lord, hearken and pity, O Lord my God, Light of the blind, and Strength of the weak; yea, also Light of those that see, and Strength of the strong: hearken unto my soul, and hear it crying out of the depths. Thy voice is my joy; thy voice exceedeth the abundance of pleasures. Give what I love: for I do love; and this hast thou given. I beseech thee by our Lord Jesus Christ, thy Son, the Man of thy right hand, the Son of Man, whom thou hast established for thyself, as thy Mediator and ours, through whom thou soughtest us, not seeking thee, but soughtest us, that we might seek thee; thy Word, through whom thou madest all things, and among them, me also; thy only begotten, through whom thou calledst to adoption the believing people, and therein me also.[2]

---

[1] Augustine, *Sermons on the Liturgical Seasons*, trans. Sarah Muldowney (New York: Fathers of the Church, 1959), 3–9.
[2] *The Confessions of St. Augustine*, ed. William Shedd (Andover, MA: William Draper, 1860), 302–303.

Day 6

John Wycliffe
(c. 1328–1384)

Wycliffe was a theologian of the church who spent most of his ministry in Oxford, England. He led the effort to translate the Bible from the Latin Vulgate into the first English translation of the Scriptures.

◇◇◇◇◇◇◇◇◇◇◇◇◇◇◇◇◇◇◇◇◇◇◇◇◇◇

For to us a child is born (Isaiah 9:6).

According to the joy that Paul declares, we may say on Christmas day, that a child is born to us; for Jesus Christ, by our belief, is this day born. And to this intent spoke God, both in figure and in letter, that a child is born to us, in whom we should have this joy. And three short words are to be spoken from Isaiah's speech, so that men may go after joy in the service of this child. First, we believe, that since our first elders had sinned, there must satisfaction be made therefore, by the righteousness of God. For as God is merciful, so he is full of righteousness. But how should he judge all the world unless he kept righteousness therein? For the Lord against whom this sin was done, is God almighty, and all righteousness; and no sin may be done but it is done against God. And ever the greater the lord is, against whom sin is done, ever the more is the sin to be recompensed of this lord. It would be great sin to do against the king's bidding; but the sin is more without measure, to do against God's bidding. According to our belief, God commanded Adam not to eat of the apple; but he broke God's command; and he was not excused, neither by his own folly (or weakness), nor by Eve, nor by the serpent. And thus by the righteousness of God, this sin must always be punished; his justice will not allow but that each trespass be punished, either on earth or in hell. And God may not accept a person to forgive his sin without satisfaction; else he must give free leave to men and to angels for to sin. And then sin would not be sin, and our God would not be God. And this is the first lesson that we take from our faith.

The second teaching that we hold that he who should make satisfaction for the sin of our first father, must needs be God and man. For as mankind trespassed, so must mankind make satisfaction. And therefore it could not be that an angel should make satisfaction for man; for neither has he the might, nor was his the person (or nature) that sinned here. But since all men are one person, that person makes satisfaction for man, if any member of this person make satisfaction for all this person. And by this may we see that if God made a man of nothing, or anew, to be of the kind of Adam, yet he were holden to God, as much as he might for himself, and so he might not make satisfaction for himself, and for Adam's sin. And thus since satisfaction must be made for Adam's sin, as it is said, such a person must make this satisfaction as was both God and man; for the worthiness of this person's deeds were even with the unworthiness of the sin.

The third teaching that needs must follow of these two, is, that a Child is born to man, to make satisfaction for man's sin. And this Child must be God and man given to man. And he must bear his empire upon his shoulder, and suffer for man. And this Child is Jesus Christ, who was born today. And we suppose that this Child is only born to those men that follow him in manner of living, for he was born against others. Those men that are unjust and proud, and rebel against God, have their judgement in Christ, that they must be condemned by him; and always, if they are unkind against his Spirit, to their death.

And thus, if we truly desire that this Child be born to us, have we joy of this Child, and we follow him in three virtues; in righteousness, and meekness, and patience for our God. For whoever condemns Christ unto his death, against the Spirit, must needs be condemned of this Child, as all others shall be saved. And thus the joy of this Child, that was thus meek and full of virtues, should make men be little in malice, and then they hold well the feast. To them that will fight and chide, I say, that this Child who is born, is Prince of peace, and loves peace; and condemns men contrary who are contrary to peace. Study we how Christ came in the fulness of time when he should; and how he came in meekness, as his birth teaches us; and how he came in patience from his birth to his death; and follow we him in these three, for joy that we have of him. For this joy, in this patience, (of Christ,) brings joy that shall last forever.[1]

Prayer from the translation of the Bible by John Wycliffe

Blissid that cometh in the name of the Lord. My God thou art, and I shal knouleche to thee; my God thou art, and I shal enhaunce thee. I steal knoldechen to thee, for thou hast ful out herd me; and thou art maad to me in to heithe. Knoulecheth to the Lord, for he is good; for in to the world the merci of hym (Psalm 118:26, 28–29).[2] [Blessed is he who comes in the name of the Lord. My God, you are, and I shall acknowledge you; my God, you are, and I shall exalt you. I shall acknowledge you, for you have fully heard me; and you have been made into my salvation. Acknowledge the Lord, for he is good; for his mercy endures forever.]

---

[1] John Wycliff, *Writings of the Reverend and Learned John Wickliff* (London: The Religious Tract Society, 1831), 186–187.
[2] *The Holy Bible, in the Earliest English Versions by John Wycliffe*, Vol. 2, ed. Josiah Foshall and Frederic Madden (Oxford: University Press, 1850), 859.

Day 7

Martin Luther
(1483-1546)

Luther was a pastor and theologian who ministered in Wittenberg, Germany. Instrumental in the Reformation, he is known for his preaching, his work of translating the Bible into German, founding the Lutheran Church and writing the *Ninety-Five Theses*, the Lutheran *Small Catechism* and *Bondage of the Will*.

◇◇◇◇◇◇◇◇◇◇◇◇◇◇◇◇◇◇◇◇◇◇◇◇◇

But when the fullness of time had come, God sent forth his Son, born of woman, born under the law, to redeem those who were under the law, so that we might receive adoption as sons (Galatians 4:4-5).

Note how Paul defines Christ's person and work. His person consists of his divine and human nature (God sent his Son, born of a woman). Christ, therefore, is truly God and truly human. Paul in this letter is dealing with the highest matter of all—namely, the gospel, faith, Christian righteousness and the person and office of Christ, what Christ has taken upon himself and done for us, and what benefits he has brought to us wretched sinners. But how has Christ redeemed us? This is how: he was born under law. When Christ came, he found us all captives under governors and imprisoned by the law. Although he is Lord of the law, so that the law has no authority over him (for he is the Son of God), he makes himself subject to the law. Here the law executes upon him all the jurisdiction it has over us. It accuses and terrifies us; it makes us subject to sin, death and the wrath of God and condemns us with its sentence. And it has a perfect right so to do, for we are all sinners (Ephesians 2:3). On the other hand, Christ "committed no sin, neither was deceit found in his mouth" (1 Peter 2:22). Therefore, he was not subject to the law. Yet the law was no less cruel against this innocent, righteous and blessed Lamb than it was against us cursed and damned sinners. In fact, it was more rigorous, for it made him guilty before God of the sins of the whole world; it so terrified and oppressed him with heaviness and anguish of spirit that his sweat was like drops of blood (Luke 22:44). The law condemned him to death, the death of the cross. This was indeed an amazing combat, in that the law, which was created, gave such an assault to its Creator and, against all right and equity, exerts over the Son of God the whole tyranny that it exercises over us children of wrath. Now, therefore, because the law so cursedly sinned against its God, it is accused and arraigned. Christ says, "Law, you mighty queen and cruel regent over mankind, what have I done that you should accuse me, terrify me and condemn me who am innocent?" Now the law, which had already condemned and killed everyone, when it has nothing with which to defend itself, is so condemned and vanquished that it loses its whole right, not only over Christ, but also over all those who believe in him; for to those people Christ says, "'Come to me, all you who are weary and burdened' by the yoke of the law (Matthew 11:28). I could have overcome the law by my absolute power, without suffering myself; for I am the Lord of the law, and therefore it has no rights over me. But I have made myself subject to the law for the sake of you who were under the law, putting on your flesh. In my own inestimable love I humbled and yielded myself to the same prison, tyranny and bondage of the law under which you served as captives. I allowed the law to have dominion over me, its Lord, to terrify me and make me captive to sin, death and the wrath of God, which it ought not to have done. Therefore, I have vanquished the law by double right and authority—first, as the Son of God and Lord of the law, and, second, in your person. It is as though you had overcome the law yourselves, for my victory is yours."

Thus Paul speaks everywhere of this marvelous combat between Christ and the law; and to make matters clearer, he describes the law as being like a mighty person who had condemned and killed Christ, and whom Christ, overcoming death, had conquered, condemned and killed (Ephesians 2:14; 4:8; Psalm 68; Romans 8:3). By this victory Christ banished the law from our conscience, so that now it can no longer confound us in God's sight or drive us to despair or condemn us. Indeed, it continues to reveal our sin, to accuse and terrify us, but the conscience takes hold of these words of the apostle that Christ has redeemed us from the law and is raised up by faith and receives great comfort. Thanks be therefore to God, who has given us the victory, through our Lord Jesus Christ.[1]

Prayer of Martin Luther

Behold, Lord, an empty vessel that needs to be filled. My Lord, fill it. I am weak in the faith; strengthen thou me. I am cold in love; warm me and make me fervent that my love may go out to my neighbour. I do not have a strong and firm faith; at times I doubt and am unable to trust thee altogether. O Lord, help me. Strengthen my faith and trust in thee. In thee I have sealed the treasures of all I have. I am poor; thou art rich and didst come to be merciful to the poor. I am a sinner; thou art upright. With me there is an abundance of sin; in thee is the fulness of righteousness. Therefore, I will remain with thee of whom I can receive but to whom I may not give. Amen.[2]

---

[1] Martin Luther, *Galatians* (Wheaton, IL: Crossway, 1998), 199–201.
[2] Clyde Manschreck, *Prayers of the Reformers* (London: The Epworth Press, 1958), 79.

Day 8

John Calvin
(1509-1564)

Calvin was a pastor, theologian and prolific author, who ministered from Geneva, Switzerland and wrote many commentaries, tracts, treatises, sermons and letters, particularly his *Institutes of the Christian Religion*. He was instrumental in establishing the Protestant Reformation throughout Europe.

◇◇◇◇◇◇◇◇◇◇◇◇◇◇◇◇◇◇◇◇◇◇◇◇◇◇◇

Great indeed, we confess, is the mystery of godliness:
He was manifested in the flesh, vindicated by the Spirit,
seen by angels, proclaimed among the nations, believed on in
the world, taken up in glory (1 Timothy 3:16).

Let us mark well the words that are here used by Paul: God was manifest in the flesh. When he calls Jesus Christ *God*, he admits this nature which he had before the world was made. It is true, there is but one God, but in this one essence we must comprehend the Father, and a wisdom which cannot be severed from him, and an everlasting virtue, which always was, and shall forever be in him. Thus, Jesus Christ was true God! As he was the wisdom of God before the world was made, and before eternity. It is said, he was made manifest in the flesh. By the word *flesh*, Paul gives us to understand that he was true man, and took upon him our nature. By the word *manifest*, he shows that in him there were two natures. But we must not think that there is one Jesus Christ which is God, and another Jesus Christ which is man! But we must know him only as God and man. Let us so distinguish the two natures which are in him, that we may know that the Son of God is our brother.

Paul adds, he was "vindicated by the Spirit." The word *vindicated*, is oftentimes used in Scripture, for *approved*. When it is said, he was vindicated, it is not that he became vindicated, it is not that he was acquitted by men, as though they were his judges, and he bound to give them an account: no, no; there is no such thing; but it is when the glory is given him which he deserves, and we confess him to be what indeed he really is. It is said, the gospel is vindicated when men receive it obediently, and through faith submit themselves to the doctrine that God teaches: so in this place, it is said, Jesus Christ was vindicated in the Spirit.

We must not content ourselves by looking at the bodily presence of Jesus Christ, which was visible, but we must look higher. John says, "God was made flesh"; or the Word of God, which is the same. The Word of God, which was God before the creation of the world, was made flesh; that is, was united to our nature: so that the Son of the virgin Mary, is God; yea, the everlasting God! His infinite power was there manifested; which is a sure witness that he is the true God!

When we hear this Word, mystery, let us remember two things; first, that we learn to keep under our senses, and flatter not ourselves that we have sufficient knowledge and ability to comprehend so vast a matter. In the second place, let us learn to climb up beyond ourselves, and reverence that majesty which passes our understanding. We must not be sluggish nor drowsy but think upon this doctrine, and endeavour to become instructed therein. When we have acquired some little knowledge thereof, we should strive to profit thereby, all the days of our life. When we become possessed of this knowledge, that the Son of God is joined to us, we should cast our eyes upon that which is so highly set forth in him that is, the virtue and power of the Holy Spirit. So then, Jesus Christ did not only appear as man, but showed indeed that he was almighty God, as all the fulness of the Godhead dwelt in him. If we once know this, we may well perceive, that it is not without cause that Paul says, all the treasures of wisdom are hidden in our Lord Jesus Christ [Colossians 2:3].

When we have once laid hold on the promises of this Mediator, we shall know the height and depth, the length and breadth, yes, and whatsoever is necessary for our salvation: so that we may stay our faith upon him, as upon the only true God; and likewise behold him as our brother; who hath not only come near to us, but hath united and joined himself to us in such a manner, that he hath become the same substance. If we have come to this, let us know that we have arrived to the perfection of wisdom, which is spoken of by Paul in another place (1 Corinthians 2:6), that we may fully rejoice in the goodness of God; for it hath pleased him to lighten us with the brightness of his gospel, and to draw us into his heavenly kingdom.[1]

Prayer of John Calvin

Grant, almighty God, that we may diligently consider in how many ways we are bound to thee, and may deservedly magnify thy fatherly goodness toward us, so that in return we may desire to devote ourselves to thee: Grant also, that as thou hast adorned us with thy glory, we may endeavour to glorify thy name, until at length we arrive at the enjoyment of that eternal glory which thou hast prepared for us in heaven through Christ our Lord. Amen.[2]

---

[1] *A Selection of the Most Celebrated Sermons of John Calvin* (New York: S. & D.A. Forbes, 1830), 25, 31–34.
[2] Clyde Manschreck, *Prayers of the Reformers* (London: The Epworth Press, 1958), 7.

Day 9

Catherine Parr
(1512-1548)

Catherine was the Queen of England and Ireland and the last wife of King Henry VIII. Through her writings and her education of her stepchildren Elizabeth and Edward, she influenced the English Reformation. She was the first woman to publish a work in her own name, the bestselling *Prayers or Meditations*.

◇◇◇◇◇◇◇◇◇◇◇◇◇◇◇◇◇◇◇◇◇◇◇◇◇◇◇◇

Christ Jesus, who, though he was in the form of God, did not count equality with God a thing to be grasped, but emptied himself, by taking the form of a servant, being born in the likeness of men (Philippians 2:5-7).

Let us therefore now, I pray you, by faith, behold and consider the great charity and goodness of God, in sending his Son to suffer death for our redemption when we were his mortal enemies; and after what sort and manner he sent him. First, it is to be considered, yea, to be undoubtedly and with a perfect faith believed, that God sent him to us freely; for he did give him, and sold him not. A more noble and rich gift he could not have given. He sent not a servant or a friend, but his only Son, so dearly beloved; not in delights, riches and honours, but in crosses, poverties and slanders; not as a Lord, but as a servant, yes, and, in most vile and painful sufferings, to wash us, not with water, but with his own precious blood; not from mire, but from the puddle and filth of our iniquities. He hath given him not to make us poor, but to enrich us with his divine virtues, merits and graces; yea, and in him he hath given us all good things, and finally himself, and with such great charity as cannot be expressed. Was it not a most high and abundant love of God to send Christ to shed his blood, to lose honour, life and all for his enemies? Even in the time when we had done him most injury he first showed his charity to us with such flames of love, that greater could not be showed. God in Christ hath opened unto us, although we are weak and blind of ourselves, that we may behold in this miserable estate the great wisdom, goodness and truth, with all the other godly perfections which are in Christ. Therefore inwardly to behold Christ crucified upon the cross is the best and goodliest meditation that can be. We may see also in Christ crucified the beauty of the soul better than in all the books of the world: for who that with a lively faith sees and feels in spirit that Christ, the Son of God, is dead for the satisfying and purifying of the soul, shall see that his soul is appointed for the very tabernacle and mansion of the inestimable and incomprehensible majesty and honour of God. We see also in Christ crucified how vain and foolish the world is, and how that Christ, being most wise, despised the same. We see also how blind it is, because the same knows not Christ, but persecutes him. We see also how unkind the world is, by the killing of Christ in the time he did show it most favour. How hard and obstinate was it that would not be mollified with so many tears, such sweat, and so much bloodshed of the Son of God, suffering with such great and high love? Therefore he is now very blind who sees not how vain, foolish, false, ingrate, cruel, hard, wicked and evil the world is. We may also in Christ crucified weigh our sins, as in a divine balance, how grievous and how weighty they are, seeing they have crucified Christ; for they would never have been counterpoised but with the great and precious weight of the blood of the Son of God. And therefore God, of his high goodness, determined that his blessed Son should rather suffer bloodshed than our sins should have condemned us. We shall never know our own misery and wretchedness but with the light of Christ crucified; then we shall see our own cruelty, when we feel his mercy; our own unrighteousness and iniquity, when we see his righteousness and holiness. Therefore, to learn to know truly our own sins is to study in the book of the crucifix, by continual conversation in faith; and to have perfect and plentiful charity is to learn, first by faith, the charity that is in God toward us. We may see also in Christ upon the cross how great the pains of hell, and how blessed the joys of heaven are; and what a sharp and painful thing it shall be to them that shall be deprived of that sweet, happy and glorious joy, Christ. Then this crucifix is the book wherein God hath included all things, and hath most compendiously written therein all truth profitable and necessary for our salvation. Therefore let us endeavour ourselves to study this book, that we, being enlightened with the Spirit of God, may give him thanks for so great a benefit.[1]

Prayer of Catherine Parr

O everlasting Light, far passing all things, send down the beams of thy brightness from above, and purify and lighten the inward parts of my heart. Quicken my soul and all the powers thereof, that it may cleave fast, and be joined to thee, in joyful gladness of spiritual desires. Teach me, Lord, to fulfil thy will, to live meekly and worthily before thee, for thou art all my wisdom and knowledge, thou art he that knowest me as I am, that knewest me before the world was made, and before I was born or brought into this life. To thee, O Lord, be honour, glory and praise, for ever and ever. Amen.[2]

---

[1] *British Reformers: Writings of Edward the Sixth, William Hugh, Queen Catherine Parr, Anne Askew, Lady Jane Grey, Hamilton, and Balnaves*, ed. William Engles (Philadelphia: Presbyterian Board of Publication, 1842), 213–214.
[2] Engles, ed., *British Reformers*, 193, 199.

Day 10

Richard Sibbes
(1577-1635)

Sibbes was a London pastor and Cambridge theologian known for his Puritan beliefs, Christ-centred preaching and devotional books, *The Bruised Reed*, *Glorious Freedom: The Excellency of the Gospel above the Law* and *The Tender Heart*.

◇◇◇◇◇◇◇◇◇◇◇◇◇◇◇◇◇◇◇◇◇◇◇◇◇◇◇

Therefore the Lord himself will give you a sign. Behold, the virgin shall conceive and bear a son, and shall call his name Immanuel (Isaiah 7:14).

The Jews at this time were in a distressed condition by reason of the siege of two kings, Resin and Pekah; the one the king of Syria, the other the king of Israel. And so the prophet seeks to comfort them, and tells them that these two kings were but as two fire-brands, that should consume themselves and then go out. For confirmation of this (because he saw the heart both of king and people astonished,) he bids them, "Ask a sign of anything in heaven and earth" (verse 11). "No," said King Ahaz, "I will not tempt God," and making religion his pretense against religion, (being a most wilful and wicked man) would not. The prophet in holy indignation for the refusing of a sign, declares, "Therefore the Lord himself will give you a sign."

What is that? "The virgin shall conceive and bear a son, and shall call his name Immanuel." From the inference, we may see the conflict between the infinite goodness of God and the inflexible stubbornness of man. God's goodness striving with man's wickedness, his goodness overcomes and triumphs over the contention of man's sinful strivings: his mercy prevails against man's malice.

This was not so much a sign for the present as a promise of a miraculous benefit which was to be presented almost 800 years after the prophet spoke these words—even the incarnation of Christ, a miracle of miracles, a benefit of benefits and the cause of all benefits. He brings comfort against the present distress from a benefit to come. And to show how this can be a ground of comfort, at this time of distress, that a virgin shall conceive; we must know, that Christ was the Lamb slain from the beginning of the world (Revelation 13:8). All the godly of the Jews knew it well enough, the Messiah being all their comfort, they knew that he was yesterday and today, and shall be the same forever [Hebrews 13:8]. The church had in all times comfort from Christ. And thus the prophet applies the comfort to the house of David. And therefore the house of David shall not be extinct and dissolved. The reason is strong: you of the house of David are in fear that your kingdom and nation shall be destroyed; but know that the Messiah must come of a virgin, and of the house of David. And considering this must certainly come to pass, why do you fear?

Again it has this force of reason: The promise of our Messiah is the grand promise of all, and the cause of all promises, for all promises made to the church, are either promises of Christ himself, or promises in him, and for his sake, because he takes all promises from God and conveys them, and makes them good to us.

Now the reason stands thus: If God will give a Messiah, that shall be the son of a virgin, and Immanuel, certainly he will give you deliverance. He that will do the greater, will do the lesser; what is the deliverance you desire to the promised deliverance from hell and damnation, and to the benefit by the Messiah, which you profess to hope for, and believe? The apostle himself reasons thus: "He who did not spare his own Son but gave him up for us all, how will he not also with him graciously give us all things?" (Romans 8:32). If God will give Christ to be Immanuel and incarnate, he will not stand upon any other inferior promises or mercies whatsoever. Let it be our comfort, that God is Immanuel, he left heaven, and took our nature to bring us there, where he himself is. When times of dissolution come, consider, I am now going to him to heaven, that came down from there, to bring me to that eternal mansion of rest and glory. God became man, that he might make man like God, partaking of his divine nature, in grace here, and glory hereafter. Shall not I go to him that suffered so much for me? Therefore says Paul, "My desire is to depart and be with Christ" (Philippians 1:23), which is the effect of Christ's prayer, "Father," he says, "my will is, that where I am, they may be also" (John 14:3). And in this God hears Christ, that all that believe in him shall be where Christ is; as he came from heaven to be where we are. Lay up these things in your hearts, that so you may receive benefit by them.[1]

Prayer of Richard Sibbes

O Lord! Christ which thou gavest me is the righteousness which thou canst not but accept, seeing his righteousness is infinite, and thou hast made it mine. I am a beggar of myself, but thou hast made Christ all in all to me, to that end that thou mayest esteem of us all in all to thee. Oh how quiet and peaceable is that soul that is in this estate.[2]

---

[1] Richard Sibbes, *A Miracle of Miracles* (London: John Rothwell, 1638), 1–5, 25.
[2] Richard Sibbes, *Complete Works*, vol. VII (Edinburgh: James Nicol, 1864), 260.

Day 11

Jeremiah Burroughs
(1599-1646)

Burroughs was a Puritan pastor and popular preacher in London, and a part of the Westminster Assembly. He is most known for his work *The Rare Jewel of Christian Contentment*.

"For God so loved the world, that he gave his only Son, that whoever believes in him should not perish but have eternal life" (John 3:16).

The first and principal thing in the gospel, is the holding forth unto us the infinite love of God to mankind; this is the very end of the gospel, that God might declare what an infinite love he has for the children of men, yes, for men rather than for angels. You know that Scripture in John 3:16. And indeed that one verse has more of God in it than all creatures in heaven and earth. It is as if God should say when he comes to reveal the gospel, I will have a way that it shall appear to men and angels forever what the greatness of my love is for these poor creatures, unto the children of men: And to that end I send my Son, the second Person in Trinity, to take their natures upon him, to come to be their Mediator; there will I manifest what my love is; that shall be the great fruit of love. It is the similitude of a learned divine (says he) the love of God in all other things in comparison of the love of God in Christ revealed in the gospel, it is a little spark of fire in comparison of the heat in a furnace; when a furnace is heated red hot, it may be a few sparks of fire fly out, but what is one of those sparks of fire that fly out in comparison of all the heat that there is in the furnace, all the fruits of the love of God to mankind in all the works that ever God did do, are but as that one spark only; excepting this of Christ; and the love of God unto mankind in Christ is as it were the heat of the furnace, there's burning love indeed, the love of God in Christ, this is the great scope of the gospel, the great aim of God, the great design that God had in the gospel to make known the infinitude of his love unto the children of men: Now then if so be that God in the gospel reveals what there was in his heart from all eternity to mankind (for so it is) that's the scope of the gospel; there was in the heart of God infinite love burning toward mankind, God from eternity saw mankind before him, and there was that strong inclination of his heart toward them in love, as did even burn in his heart. Now in time God reveals this in the gospel, in the doctrine thereof he opens his heart to the children of men: whenever the gospel comes to be preached in any place, God looks upon that place and has these kind of workings in himself, "Well, that love of mine that I have had burning in my bosom from all eternity toward these poor creatures, now it shall be opened, now it shall be revealed"; just as it was with Joseph that had his heart so warm in love unto his brothers, that though he kept it in a while he could not keep it in long, but at length it breaks out as fire, his heart yearned toward his brethren, and he weeps tears of love over their necks. So in the gospel of Christ, look upon God toward poor creatures, as Joseph toward his brothers, and God as it were keeping in his heart toward them for a long time; but now when the gospel comes among them God opens his very heart to them, now therefore there must be a behaviour that becomes the gospel, as becomes this great thing in the gospel, that is the chief thing indeed that the gospel holds forth in every line of it, and discovers his eternal love toward them in particular, in the Son of his love, Christ Jesus in whom he is well pleased.

God so loved the world, so dearly, as that which was the dearest thing to God he gave for a testimony of his love to mankind. The dearest thing, What's that? His Son. If God should have said, "That I might testify my love to mankind, as I have made one world for them, I will make ten thousand more, yes, I will make so many worlds as every one of the children of men shall have a world to possess;" you would think this were very much: Oh this were nothing in comparison of that expression, "God so loved the world, that he gave his only Son"; the Son of God is infinitely dearer to God than ten thousand thousand millions of worlds are.

Oh, to be always with God in the arms of Christ; it is our heaven on earth. Oh that Jesus Christ from whose hand and heart this gospel came, would now preach it home to every heart of us, that the truths thereof, may be turned into grace, spirit and life.[1]

Prayer of Jeremiah Burroughs

Oh, Lord, thou knowest the desires of our souls are that thou mayest rule over us, O when shall we hear that blessed voice, "The kingdoms of the earth are the Lord's and his Christ's, and he shall reign forevermore! Oh, that thy kingdom might come more powerfully in our hearts, and that it might be more conspicuous in church and state!"[2]

---

[1] Jeremiah Burroughs, *Gospel Conversation* (London: Peter Cole, 1653), 53–57, 62.
[2] Jeremiah Burroughs, *The Glorious Name of God, the Lord of Hosts* (London: R. Dawlman, 1643), 73.

Day 12

Isaac Ambrose
(1604 -1664)

Ambrose was a Puritan pastor in England who helped establish the Presbyterian church. He was a Christ-centred preacher and author, known for his books *The Christian Warrior* and *Looking Unto Jesus*.

◇◇◇◇◇◇◇◇◇◇◇◇◇◇◇◇◇◇◇◇◇◇◇◇

Beloved, we are God's children now, and what we will be has not yet appeared; but we know that when he appears we shall be like him, because we shall see him as he is (1 John 3:2).

Looking is either ocular, or mental. For ocular vision, in heaven, we shall look on Jesus; and we shall see him as he is, says the apostle (1 John 3:2). But till then we must walk by faith, and not by sight. For mental vision, or the inward eye, that is it which the apostle speaks of in his prayers, "having the eyes of your hearts enlightened" (Ephesians 1:18). Looking unto, is the act; but how? It is such a look as includes all these acts: knowing, considering, desiring, hoping, believing, loving, joying, enjoying of Jesus and conforming to Jesus. It is such a look as stirs up affections in the heart, and the effects thereof in our life; it is such a look as leaves a quickening and enlivening upon the spirit; it is such a look as works us into a warm affection, raised resolution, a holy and upright way of life. Consider, that a thorough sight of Christ, will increase your inward joy in Christ, "Your father Abraham rejoiced that he would see my day. He saw it and was glad" (John 8:56). A right sight of Christ, will make a right-sighted Christian glad at heart; I wonder not that you walk uncomfortably, if you never tried this art of Christ-contemplation. Can you have comfort from Christ, and never think of Christ? Does anything in the world gladden you, when you do not remember it? If you were possessed of all the treasure in the earth, if you had title to the highest dignities, and never thought of them, sure they would never bring you joy. Come look up unto Jesus, fix your eyes, thoughts, and hearts on that blessed object, and then you may expect David's experience, "My mouth will praise you with joyful lips" (Psalm 63:5). A frequent access to Christ in a way of meditation cannot but warm the soul in spiritual comforts. When the sun in the spring draws near our part of the earth, how do all things congratulate its approach? The earth looks green, the trees shoot forth, the plants revive, the birds sing sweetly, the face of all things smiles upon us and all the creatures below rejoice. Christians! If you would but draw near, and look on this Sun of Righteousness, Jesus Christ, what a spring of joy would be within you? How would your graces be fresh and green? How would you forget your winter sorrows? How early would you rise (as those birds in the spring) to sing the praise of our great Creator, and dear Redeemer.

Consider that your eye on Jesus will preserve the vigour of all your graces. As the body is apt to be changed into the state of the air it breaths in, and the food it lives on, so will your spirits receive an alteration according to the objects which they are exercised about. You that complain of deadness and dullness, that you cannot love Christ, nor rejoice in his loves, that you have no life in prayer, nor any other duty, and yet you never tried this enlivening course, or at least you were careless and inconstant in it; what, are not you the cause of your own complaints? "Is not your life hid with Christ in God?" O! whither must you go but to Christ for it? If you would have light and heat, why then are you not more in the Sunshine? If you would have more of that grace which flows from Christ, why are you no more with Christ for it? For want of this recourse to Jesus Christ, your souls are as candles that are not lighted, and your duties are as sacrifices which have no fire; fetch one coal daily from this Altar, and see if your offerings will not burn; keep close to this reviving Fire, and see if your affections will not warm. Surely if there be any comfort of hope, if any flames of love, if any life of faith, if any vigour of dispositions, if any motions toward God, if any meltings of a softened heart, they flow from here; men are apt to bewail their want of desire, and hope, and joy, and faith, and love to Jesus Christ, while this very duty would nourish all these. Consider, your hearts should be on Christ, when the heart of Christ is so much on you. Christ is our Friend, and in that respect he loves us, and bears us in his heart; and shall not he be ours? Does he not bear you continually in the arms of love, and promise that all shall work together for your good [Romans 8:28]? Every thought of Jesus is sweet and pleasant, nay, it's better than wine; "We will extol your love more than wine" (Song of Songs 1:4).[1]

Prayer of Isaac Ambrose

O Lord, thou hast looked on my low estate, and visited me with mercy from on high; of a stranger and foreigner, thou hast made me a free citizen of the New Jerusalem: Now I see, I read it in thy precious promises, that my name is registered in heaven; an eternal weight of glory is reserved for me; heaven is my home, my hope, my inheritance: O where should my heart be, but where my hope is? Now all glory, and honour and praise be given to my God! O the incomprehensible love and favour of my dear Lord! What a mercy is this! What promises are these? My soul rejoyceth in thee my God, my spirit shall bless thy name forever and ever.[2]

---

[1] Isaac Ambrose, *Looking unto Jesus*, Vol. 1 (James Ormiston: Edinburgh, 1723), 13–26.
[2] Isaac Ambrose, *The Compleat Works of that Eminent Minister of God's Word, Mr. Isaac Ambrose* (London Kingdom: R. C, B. T, G. S, 1701), 146.

Day 13

John Flavel
(c. 1627-1691)

Flavel was a Puritan Presbyterian pastor in England whose writings influenced future pastors such as Jonathan Edwards, George Whitefield, Robert Murray M'Cheyne and Andrew Bonar. His *Works* include *The Mystery of Providence* and *Navigation Spiritualized*.

And the Word became flesh and dwelt among us, and we have seen his glory, glory as of the only Son from the Father, full of grace and truth (John 1:14).

You have heard the covenant of redemption opened. The work therein propounded by the Father, and consented to by the Son, is such as infinitely exceeds the power of any mere creature to perform. He that undertakes to satisfy God, by obedience for man's sin, must himself be *God*; and he that performs such a perfect obedience, by doing, and suffering all that the law required, in our room, must be *man*. These two natures must be united in one Person, else there could not be a concourse or co-operation of either nature in his mediatory works. How these natures are united, in the wonderful person of our Immanuel, is the first part of the great mystery of godliness: a subject studied and adored by angels! And the mystery thereof is wrapped up in this text. Hence note, that Jesus Christ did really assume the true and perfect nature of man, into a personal union with his divine nature, and still remains true God, and true man, in one Person forever. The proposition contains one of the deepest mysteries of godliness (1 Timothy 3: 16). A mystery, by which apprehension is dazzled, invention astonished and all expression swallowed up. If ever the tongues of angels were desirable to explicate any word of God, they are so here. Great is the interest of words in this doctrine. We walk upon the brink of danger. The least tread awry may engulf us in the bogs of error. But this assumption of which I speak, is that whereby the second Person in the Godhead did take the human nature into a personal union with himself, by virtue whereof the manhood subsists in the second Person, yet without confusion, both making but one Person, Immanuel, God with us.

So that though we truly ascribe a two-fold nature to Christ, yet not a double person; for the human nature of Christ never subsisted separately and distinctly, by any personal subsistence of its own, as it does in all other men, but from the first moment of conception, subsisted in union with the second Person.

The divine did not assume the human nature necessarily, but voluntarily; not out of poverty, but bounty; not because it was to be perfected by it, but to perfect it, by causing it to lie as a pipe, to the infinite all-filling fountain of grace and glory, of which it is the great receptacle. And so, consequently, to qualify and prepare him for a full discharge of his mediatorship, in the offices of our Prophet, Priest and King. Had he not this double nature in the unity of his Person, he could not have been our Prophet: For, as God, he knows the mind and will of God (John 1:18; 3:13), and as man he is fitted to impart it suitably to us (Deuteronomy 18:15–18; Acts 3:22). As Priest, had he not been man, he could have shed no blood; and if not God, it had been no adequate value for us (Hebrews 2:17; Acts 3:28). As King, had he not been man, he would have been dissimilar, and so no fit head for us. And if not God, he could neither rule nor defend his body, the church.

Hence we see, to what a height God intends to build up the happiness of man, in that he has laid the foundation of it so deep, in the incarnation of his own Son. They that intend to build high, use to lay the foundation low. The happiness and glory of our bodies, as well as souls, are founded in Christ's taking our flesh upon him: for, therein, as in a model or pattern, God intended to show what in time he resolves to make of our bodies; for he will transform our vile bodies, and make them one day conformable to the glorious body of Jesus Christ (Philippians 3:21). God and man in one Person! Oh! thrice happy conjunction! As man, he is full of experimental sense of our infirmities, wants and burdens; and, as God, he can support and supply them all. The aspect of faith upon this wonderful Person, how relieving, how reviving, how abundantly satisfying is it? God will never divorce the believing soul, and its comfort, after he has married our nature to his own Son, by the hypostatical, and our persons also, by the blessed mystical union.[1]

Prayer of John Flavel

O melting consideration, that the Lord of glory should manifest himself in the likeness of sinful flesh; and not only so, but choose such a state of outward meanness and poverty. O Jesus, by how much the viler thou madest thyself for me, by so much the dearer shalt thou be to me.[2]

---

[1] John Flavel, *The Whole Works of John Flavel*, Vol. 1 (London: W. Baynes and Son, 1820), 72–85.
[2] John Flavel, *The Select Works of the Rev. John Flavel*, ed. G.B. (London: Frederick Mason, 1834), 82.

Day 14

Catharina Regina von Greiffenberg
(1633-1694)

Von Greiffenberg was an Austrian poet and suffered persecution from the Habsburgs as a Protestant Lutheran. She devoted her life to glorifying God through her poetry. Her best known collection of poetry is called in English *Spiritual Sonnets, Songs, and Poems*.

And Mary said, "My soul magnifies the Lord, and my spirit rejoices in God my Savior" (Luke 1:46-47).

My spirit, spurred by the Holy Spirit, leaps for joy in God my Saviour; it trembles, jumps, raves, praises and exults with joy and ardent longing to love and praise in no other way than when the flame makes water boil so that the bright bubbles leap up and rise out of and above the vessel and do not suffer themselves to be stilled or damped. Thus joy effervesces and rises up in my spirit, which makes the sweetness of God's grace overflow from the heat; I feel a joy that my heart is too small to contain, since this joy is the sort that makes the pomegranate burst and split thus that the kernels of love can be seen therein.

The joy that is in me forces me out of myself, for what remains within itself and master of itself is no true joy of the spirit. The proper joy of the spirit effervesces, flames, flies, rises, and sends smoke up to heaven; it renders one drunk in heavenly ecstasy so that in the spirit one reels, dances, leaps and shouts for joy, and knows not how to contain oneself. One is not in control of oneself; instead one suffers the Omnipotent One to hold sway in one's weakness. One is not frightened of the world, because one has the Ruler of it in one's heart whence all the little spirits, blood vessels, and drops of blood come forth, like fireworks when they have been lighted and are to catch fire and burst into a million sparks of praise.

This single spirit inspires thousands and thousands of flames of joy: now a rocket of the eternal joy of heaven goes off, now a fire of joy flies up over God's glory; there a ground rocket over the love of Jesus; here a sun-burst over the force of the Holy Spirit; on the one hand, a ball of jubilation over the creation of the world, on the other hand, a burning time-fuse over the wondrous rule; there a spark of thanks leaps into the air, here a mine that scatters in a thousand stars of praise. The mercies promised for the future drive the brightest little stars of praise to such heights that they seem to compete with the fixed or static stars in the eighth heaven.

The glorious and holy joy of the spirit is an inextinguishable light in all the abysses of the sea and the waters of heaven. Oh! The glorious heavenly fire of joy of the Holy Spirit—how it ignites and transfixes me so that for joy I cannot describe the joy. 1 rejoice not merely from the prompting of nature or the spirit but rather from the greatest cause in the world, namely, in and over God, my Saviour. I rejoice in God who is in me and over God who is under my heart. I rejoice in him who is a vessel of all joys and who is now contained by my body (when he is otherwise unconstrained); in him who, to gain eternal joy for the entire world, takes on within me the capacity to experience sorrow so as to deliver us from all sorrow.

My spirit rejoices in God, my Saviour, who takes from me the tool of my own salvation, for I as well as others will be saved through his powerful suffering and death. Oh! I rejoice infinitely on this account over the ineffable grace of God that from me (who, myself born of Adam, would have been damned) took the means, matter and tool by which I and all of the children of Adam will be saved. Oh! Should I not rejoice that he who is one with God the Father is also of one flesh and blood with me, that I am to be the mother of the One of whom God is the Father, that within me the Creator of my body is provided with a body, that I can embrace the one who embraces everything, conceive the inconceivable, and with my weak body encompass the One who encompasses heaven and earth, that I carry in my body the One who carries heaven and earth, me, and all things?

Oh, joy above all joy! The source of the first living beings takes on a new being within me to gain for us living joy and salvation. What bliss to give from my body a body to the One who is a lord of all spirits! What unimaginable joy to have the Spirit in heaven and God in my body; to see, nay, feel my insignificance; to become a casket of the sum of everything; and to place upon him a nature that even in death and in all eternity is indivisible, a nature by which our sinful nature would be purified and made holy.[1]

Prayer of Catharina Regina von Greiffenberg

O thou omnipotent God-with-us! Be with us too in gratitude! Free those hearts that thou redeemest from hell [and] from the hellish vice of ingratitude as well! Thou who hast gained heaven for us, give us the fruit of heaven too for which to be grateful to thee! Thou hast already given me the will. Give me also the fulfilment! Since my misery pulled thee from heaven, pull my weakness heavenward again with thy fulfilment. When it is a matter of the will, there is none more ardent and eager in nature and among all living creatures than my will to thank and serve thee. I feel more thoughts of thanks in me than I can utter, yet certainly even more

---

[1] Catharina Regina von Greiffenberg, *Meditations on the Incarnation, Passion, and Death of Jesus Christ*, ed. and trans. Lynne Tatlock (Chicago: University of Chicago Press, 2010), 217–220.

cause [for giving thanks], which causes me to wish my soul out of my body and up to God in heaven to be able properly to praise the God-with-us on earth, indeed, in heaven and on earth.[2]

---

[2] von Greiffenberg, *Meditations on the Incarnation*, 272.

Day 15

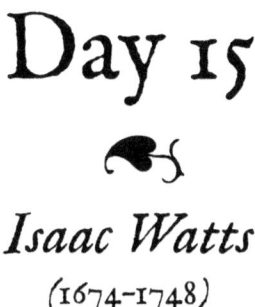

Isaac Watts
(1674-1748)

Watts was an English pastor, theologian and hymn writer, influencing churches in both England and America to adopt the singing of hymns in the Sunday service. Some of his most loved hymns are "Joy to the World," "When I Survey the Wondrous Cross," "I Sing the Mighty Power of God" and "O God, Our Help in Ages Past."

◇◇◇◇◇◇◇◇◇◇◇◇◇◇◇◇◇◇◇◇◇◇◇◇◇◇◇◇◇

For you know the grace of our Lord Jesus Christ, that though he was rich, yet for your sake he became poor, so that you by his poverty might become rich (2 Corinthians 8:9).

Among all the hearts that God ever made there have never been but three entirely free from this stain and poison; two of them were the hearts of Adam and Eve in the day of their innocence, and happy had it been for us, if pride had never found an entrance there. The third was the heart of the man Jesus, who is God's most beloved Son. It was amazing humility indeed in this glorious Person, the Son of God, that he would condescend to be born a Son of man, that he should leave the bosom of the Father and all the glories there, to dwell in flesh and blood. And when he entered our world there was nothing round him but the signs of humiliation and the marks of deep abasement; he became the child of a poor maid in Galilee, he was content to be born in a stable, for there was no room for him in the house; he lay down to take his first nap in a manger, below the rank and condition of men; and as though he were a companion for lowly creatures, he borrowed his dwelling from the ox and the donkey. This was the accommodation, this the presence-chamber of the King of Israel, of the Son of God. Come let us thus contemplate the glorious humility of the blessed Jesus, the humble infancy of our adored Saviour, and let us become infants and humble.

And let it be observed here, that every instance of lowliness and poverty in the life and circumstances of the blessed Jesus was a distinct token of the humility of his soul, for it was *chosen* poverty, it was *assumed* meanness. When he was rich in the glories and splendors of his Father's court in heaven, he laid them all aside for our sakes, and became poor on earth, that through his poverty we might be made rich. What a shameful dimness and disgrace, what divine contempt has the Son of God cast on all the lustre and glory of this world, by his choice of so lowly accommodations and so poor accoutrements? What a holy disdain of all earthly grandeur and magnificence should we learn from the incarnation and the life of the holy Jesus? Even lowliness and poverty should lose their disgraceful appearances, and seem almost an admirable sort of apparel to us, when we remember they were worn by the Son of God.

Think with thyself, O my soul, what if you have not the favour of the rich, and the society of the great ones of the earth? Do you not hear the promise of the God of heaven, and feel the divine encouragement with surprising delight? "Thus says the One who is high and lifted up, who inhabits eternity, whose name is Holy: 'I dwell in the high and holy place, and also with him who is of a contrite and lowly spirit, to revive the spirit of the lowly, and to revive the heart of the contrite'" (Isaiah 57:15). The soul that is truly humble upon religious principles, when he is cast out of the company of the great and the wealthy with scorn, is a partner of the sufferings of the holy Jesus, is an imitator of his virtues, and he shall share in his sacred honours: he shall have the great and blessed God come down and dwell with him here on earth, to enrich him with grace, and he shall be raised to dwell forever in the courts of heaven with God, and with his Son Jesus, who is the Lord of glory.

Farewell then, vanity and pride! Farewell, you scenes of grandeur, you flattering and fading glories of this life! Farewell you vain and ambitious titles among my fellow-worms! Be my ears deaf and my heart dead to all the noisy pomp, to all the sounding honours of this world! Let me be a humble and a holy follower of the holy and the humble Jesus! I adore him, I love him, I would gladly be more like him. He is my divine example and my forerunner to the world of joy above; he has a crown there provided for every humble soul, a crown which, shall never fade; he has names of dignity for all his saints, but on his own sacred head are many crowns, and to his name belong superior honours. To the Lamb that was slain ascribe glory and majesty and universal blessing forever and ever.[1]

Hymn of Praise by Isaac Watts

Hosanna to the royal Son
Of David's ancient line!
His natures two, his Person one,
Mysterious and divine.
The root of David, here we find,
And offspring, are the same:
Eternity and time are joined
In our Immanuel's name.
Blest he that comes to wretched men
With peaceful news from Heaven!
Hosannas, of the highest strain,
To Christ the Lord be given.[2]

---

[1] Isaac Watts, *The Sermons and Practical Works of Isaac Watts*, Vol. 3 (London: Albion Press, 1805), 509–512.
[2] *The Psalms and Hymns of Isaac Watts*, ed. George Burder (London: C. Whittingham, 1806), 239.

Day 16

John Wesley
(1703-1791)

John Wesley was an Anglican pastor and evangelist in the First Great Awakening, used by God to bring revival in both England and America, and one of the founders of the Methodist movement. His preaching emphasized the love of God and the need for the new birth.

For if many died through one man's trespass, much more have the grace of God and the free gift by the grace of that one man Jesus Christ abounded for many (Romans 5:15).

Some have asked, "Did not God foresee that Adam would abuse his liberty? And did he not know the baneful consequences which this must naturally have on all his posterity? And why, then, did he permit that disobedience?"

First, mankind in general have gained, by the fall of Adam, a capacity of attaining more holiness and happiness on earth than it would have been possible for them to attain if Adam had not fallen. For if Adam had not fallen, Christ had not died. What is the necessary consequence of this? It is this: There could then have been no such thing as faith in God thus loving the world, giving his only Son for us men, and for our salvation. There could have been no such thing as faith in the Son of God, as "loving us and giving himself for us" (Galatians 2:20). There could have been no faith in the Spirit of God, as renewing the image of God in our hearts, as raising us from the death of sin unto the life of righteousness. And the same grand blank which was in our faith must likewise have been in our love. We might have loved the Author of our being, the Father of angels and men as our Creator and Preserver; but we could not have loved him under the nearest and dearest relation, as delivering up his Son for us all. We might have loved the Son of God, as being "the radiance of the glory of God and the exact imprint of his nature (Hebrews 1:3) but we could not have loved him as "bearing our sins in his own body on the tree" (1 Peter 2:24).

Had there been neither natural nor moral evil in the world, what must have become of patience, meekness, gentleness, longsuffering? It is manifest they could have had no being; seeing all these have evil for their object. As God's permission of Adam's fall gave all his posterity a thousand opportunities of suffering, and thereby of exercising all those passive graces which increase both their holiness and happiness; so it gives them opportunities of doing good in numberless instances; of exercising themselves in various good works, which otherwise could have had no being. And what exertions of benevolence, of compassion, of godlike mercy, had then been totally prevented!

As the more holy we are upon earth the more happy we must be (seeing there is an inseparable connection between holiness and happiness). Therefore, the fall of Adam, *First*, by giving us an opportunity of being far more holy; *Secondly*, by giving us the occasions of doing innumerable good works, which otherwise could not have been done; and, *Thirdly*, by putting it into our power to suffer for God, whereby "the Spirit of glory and of God rests upon us" (1 Peter 4:14), may be of such advantage to the children of men, even in the present life, as they will not thoroughly comprehend till they attain life everlasting.

If God had prevented the fall of man, "the Word" would never have been "made flesh;" nor had we ever "seen his glory, glory as of the only Son from the Father" (John 1:14). Those mysteries never would have been displayed, "things into which angels long to look" (1 Peter 1:12). I think this consideration swallows up all the rest, and should never be out of our thoughts. Unless "by one man judgement had come upon all men to condemnation" (Romans 5:16), neither angels nor men could ever have known "the unsearchable riches of Christ" (Ephesians 3:8). See, then, upon the whole, how little reason we have to repine at the fall of our first parent; since from here we may derive such unspeakable advantages, both in time and eternity. See how small pretense there is for questioning the mercy of God in permitting that event to take place; since therein mercy, by infinite degrees, rejoices over judgement [James 2:3].

Where then is the man that presumes to blame God for not preventing Adam's sin? Should we not rather bless him from the ground of the heart, for therein laying the grand scheme of man's redemption, and making way for that glorious manifestation of his wisdom, holiness, justice and mercy? God permitted, in order to a fuller manifestation of his wisdom, justice and mercy, by bestowing on all who would receive it an infinitely greater happiness than they could possibly have attained if Adam had not fallen. "Oh, the depth of the riches and wisdom and knowledge of God!" (Romans 11:33). Although a thousand particulars of his judgements and of his ways are unsearchable to us, and past our finding out; yet may we discern the general scheme running through time into eternity. "According to the counsel of his own will" (Ephesians 1:5) the plan he had laid before the foundation of the world, he created the parent of all mankind in his own image; and he permitted all men to be made sinners, by the disobedience of that one man, that, by the obedience of one, all who receive the free gift may be infinitely holier and happier to all eternity.[1]

Prayer of John Wesley

O God, blessed forever, we thank and praise thee for all thy benefits, for the comforts of this life and our hope of

---

[1] John Wesley, *God's Love to Fallen Man* (London: n.p., 1791), 2–12.

everlasting salvation in the life to come. We desire to have a lively sense of thy love always possessing our hearts, that may still constrain us to love thee, to obey thee, to trust in thee, to be content with the portion thy love allots unto us and to rejoice even in the midst of all the troubles of this life. Thou hast delivered thine own Son for us all. How shalt thou not with him also freely give us all things? We depend upon thee especially for the grace of thy Holy Spirit. O that we may feel it perpetually bearing us up, by the strength of our most holy faith, above all the temptations that may at any time assault us; that we may keep ourselves unspotted from the world, and may still cleave to thee in righteousness, in lowliness, purity of heart, yea, the whole mind that was in Christ. Let thy mighty power enable us to do our duty toward thee, and toward all men, with care, and diligence, and zeal, and perseverance, unto the end.[2]

---

[2] John Wesley, *The Works of the Rev. John Wesley*, Vol. 11 (London: John Mason, 1830), 247–248.

Day 17

Jonathan Edwards
(1703-1758)

Edwards was an American pastor and theologian whose preaching and writings were influential in the First Great Awakening. He is most known for *Religious Affections, A Personal Narrative, The Nature of True Virtue* and *The End for Which God Created the World,* as well as his sermon, "Sinners in the Hands of an Angry God."

We rejoice in hope of the glory of God (Romans 5:2).

There meet in Jesus Christ, infinite justice and infinite grace. As Christ is a divine person, he is infinitely holy and just, infinitely hating sin and disposed to execute well-deserved punishment for sin. He is the Judge of the world, and is the infinitely just Judge of it, and will not at all acquit the wicked, or by any means clear the guilty. And yet he is one that is infinitely gracious and merciful. Though his justice be so strict with respect to all sin, and every breach of the law, yet he has grace sufficient for every sinner, and even the chief of sinners. And it is not only sufficient for the most unworthy to show them mercy, and bestow some good upon them, but to bestow the greatest good; yes, it is sufficient to bestow all good upon them, and to do all things for them. There is no benefit or blessing that they can receive so great, but the grace of Christ is sufficient to bestow it on the greatest sinner that ever lived.

Infinite glory and the lowest humility meet in no other person but Christ. In Jesus Christ, who is both God and man, these two diverse excellencies are sweetly united. He is a Person infinitely exalted in glory and dignity. Being in the form of God, he thought it not robbery to be equal with God (Philippians 2:6). God himself says to him, "Your throne, O God, is forever and ever" (Hebrews 1:8). But however he is thus above all, yet he is lowest of all in humility. There never was so great an instance of this virtue, among either men or angels, as Jesus. None ever was so sensible of the distance between God and him, or had a heart so lowly before God, as the man Christ Jesus (Matthew 11:29). What a wonderful spirit of humility appeared in him, when he was here upon earth, in all his behaviour! In his contentment in his lowly outward condition, contentedly living in the family of Joseph the carpenter, and Mary his mother, for thirty years together, and afterward choosing outward lowliness, poverty and contempt, rather than earthly greatness; in his cheerfully sustaining the form of a servant through his whole life, and submitting to such immense humiliation at death!

There meet in the Person of Christ, the deepest reverence toward God, and equality with God. Christ, when he was here on earth, appeared full of holy reverence toward the Father: he paid the most reverential worship to him. Thus we read of his kneeling down and praying (Matthew 22:41). This became Christ, as he was one that had taken on him the human nature. But at the same time he existed in the divine nature; whereby his Person was in all respects equal to the Person of the Father. God the Father has no attribute or perfection, that the Son has not, in equal degree and equal glory. These things meet in no other Person but Jesus Christ.

There are conjoined in the Person of Christ, infinite worthiness of good, and the greatest patience under sufferings of evil. He was perfectly innocent, and deserved no suffering. He deserved nothing from God, by any guilt of his own; and he deserved no ill from men. Yes, he was not only harmless, and undeserving of suffering, but he was infinitely worthy, worthy of the infinite love of the Father, worthy of infinite and eternal happiness, and infinitely worthy of all possible esteem, love and service from all men. And yet he was perfectly patient under the greatest sufferings, that ever were endured in this world. He suffered not from his Father, for *his* faults, but *ours*; and he suffered from men not for his faults, but for those things on account of which, he was infinitely worthy of their love and honour; which made his patience the more wonderful, and the more glorious.

This admirable conjunction of excellencies appears in the acts and various passages of Christ's life. Though Christ dwelt on the earth in lowly outward circumstances, whereby his condescension and humility especially appeared, and his majesty was veiled; yet his divine dignity and glory did in many of his acts shine through the veil, and it illustriously appeared that he was, not only the Son of Man, but the great God.[1]

Prayer of Jonathan Edwards

We have seen on what design God began the course of his providence in the beginning of the generations of men; and how he has all along carried things on agreeably to the same design without ever failing; and how at last the conclusion and final issue of things are to God; and therefore may well now cry out with the apostle (Romans 9:33): "O the depth of the riches both of the wisdom and knowledge of God! How unsearchable are his judgments, and his ways past finding out!" (and verse 36), "For of him, and through him, and to him, are all things: to whom be glory forever. Amen."[2]

---

[1] Jonathan Edwards, *Sermons on Various Important Subjects* (London: Booksellers, 1795), 249–258.
[2] Jonathan Edwards, *The Works of Jonathan Edwards*, ed. Edward Hickman, Vol. 1 (London: Ball, Arnold and Co., 1840), 616.

Day 18

George Whitefield
(1714-1770)

Whitefield was an Anglican pastor and itinerant preacher in the First Great Awakening in both England and America. He helped found the Methodist movement and preached at least 18,000 times in his life, emphasizing the doctrine of justification by faith alone, along with the need for regeneration by the Holy Spirit.

◇◇◇◇◇◇◇◇◇◇◇◇◇◇◇◇◇◇◇◇◇◇◇◇◇◇◇

The LORD God said to the serpent... "I will put enmity between you and the woman, and between your offspring and her offspring; he shall bruise your head, and you shall bruise his heel" (Genesis 3:14-15).

When I read to you these words, I may address you in the language of the holy angels to the shepherds, who were watching their flocks by night, "Behold, I bring you good news of great joy" (Luke 2:10). For this is the first promise that was made of a Saviour to the apostate race of Adam. We generally look for Christ only in the New Testament; but Christianity in one sense is very near as old as the creation.

Let us take a short view of the miserable circumstances our first parents were now in. They were legally and spiritually dead—

children of wrath and heirs of hell. They had eaten the fruit, of which God had commanded them, that they should not eat. And when arraigned before God, notwithstanding their crime was so complicated, they could not be brought to confess it. What reason can be given why sentence of death should not be pronounced? All must own they are worthy to die. Nay, how can God, consistently with his justice, possibly forgive them? He had threatened, that the day they eat of the forbidden fruit, they should surely die. And yet mercy cries, "Spare these sinners, spare the work of your own hands." Behold then, wisdom contrives a scheme how God may be just, and yet be merciful; be faithful to his threatening, punish the offence, and at the same time spare the offender. An amazing scene of divine love here opens to our view, which had been from all eternity hid in the heart of God! Notwithstanding Adam and Eve were thus unhumbled and did not so much as put up one single petition for pardon, God immediately passes sentence upon the serpent, and reveals to them a Saviour.

This first promise must certainly be but dark to our first parents, in comparison of that great light which we enjoy. And yet, dark as it was, we may assure ourselves they built upon it their hopes of everlasting salvation, and by that faith were saved. By the seed of the woman, we are here to understand the Lord Jesus Christ, who, though very God of very God, was for us men and our salvation, to have body prepared for him by the Holy Spirit, and to be born of a pure virgin, and by his obedience and death make an atonement for man's transgression, and bring in an everlasting righteousness, work in them a new nature, and thereby bruise the serpent's head, that is, destroy his power and dominion over them. By the serpent's seed, we are to understand the devil and all his children, who should be permitted by God to tempt and sift his children. It is not to be doubted but Adam and Eve understood this promise in this sense, for it is plain, in the latter part of the chapter, sacrifices were instituted. For, from where did these skins come, but from beasts slain for sacrifice, of which God made them coats? We find also Abel, as well as Cain, offering sacrifice in the next chapter; and the apostle tells us they did it by faith, no doubt in this promise (Hebrews 11:4). For, unto Adam and his wife, did the Lord God make coats of skins, and clothed them, which was a remarkable type of their being clothed with the righteousness of our Lord Jesus Christ.

This promise was literally fulfilled in the Person of our Lord Jesus Christ. Satan bruised his heel, when he tempted him for forty days in the wilderness. He bruised his heel, when he raised up strong persecution against him, during the time of his public ministry. He, in a special manner, bruised his heel when our Lord complained that his soul was exceeding sorrowful, even unto death, and he sweat great drops of blood falling upon the ground, when praying in the garden. He bruised his heel, when he put it into the heart of Judas to betray him. And he bruised him yet most of all, when his emissaries nailed him to an accursed tree, and our Lord cried out, "My God, my God, why have you forsaken me?" (Matthew 27:46). Yes; in all this, the blessed Jesus, the seed of the woman, bruised Satan's accursed head—for, in that he was tempted, he was able to help those that are tempted. "With his wounds we are healed, upon him was the chastisement that brought us peace" (Isaiah 53:5).[1]

Prayer of George Whitefield

O blessed Jesus, who art a God whose compassions fail not, and in whom all the promises are yea and amen; thou that sittest between the cherubims, show thyself amongst us. Let us now see thy outgoings! O let us now taste that thou art gracious, and reveal thy almighty arm! Get thyself the victory in these poor sinners' hearts. Let not the word spoken prove like water spilt upon the ground. Send down, send down, O great High Priest, the Holy Spirit, to convince the world of sin, of righteousness, and of judgement. So will we give thanks and praise to thee O Father, thee O Son, and thee O blessed Spirit; to whom as three Persons, but one God,

---

[1] George Whitefield, *Nine Sermons* (London: J. Lewis, 1743), 36–37, 57–58, 63–66.

be ascribed, by angels and archangels, by cherubim and seraphim, and all the heavenly hosts, all possible power, might, majesty and dominion, now and for evermore. Amen, Amen, Amen.[2]

---

[2] John Gillies, *Memoirs of Rev. George Whitefield* (New Haven, CT: Whitmore & Buckingham and H. Mansfield, 1834), 51.

Day 19

John Newton
(1725–1807)

Newton was a pastor in England known for being a former slave trader turned abolitionist, who founded the Anti-Slavery Society with William Wilberforce. He wrote a collection of hymns with William Cowper, and Newton's most famous hymn is "Amazing Grace."

"Glory to God in the highest, and on earth peace among those with whom he is pleased!" (Luke 2:14)

The glory of God was manifest, was celebrated in the highest heavens, when MESSIAH was born of a woman.

The great design and effect of his appearance with regard to mankind, is peace. *On earth peace.* Man as a fallen creature is in a state of war and rebellion against his Maker. He has renounced his allegiance and dependence, is become his own end. He is now against God, disobedient to his laws and disaffected to his government. And his conscience, if not stupefied and cauterized by frequent resistance of conviction, suggests that God is against him. He feels he is not happy here, he fears he shall be miserable hereafter. This apprehension strengthens his aversion from God. And, indeed, without an express assurance from the Lord himself whom he has offended, that there is forgiveness with him, he would not only fear, but sink into despair, if he rightly understood the horrid enormity of a state of alienation from the blessed God. But infinite wisdom and mercy have provided, and propounded a method, by which the honour of the divine perfections and government are secured, and pardon and peace graciously granted to rebels. *God was in Christ reconciling the world to himself.* The knowledge of this mercy, when revealed to the sinner's heart, subdues his enmity, constrains him to throw down his arms, and to make an unreserved submission and surrender of himself; forms him to a state of love and confidence, and disposes him to habitual and cheerful obedience. Now *mercy and truth are met together, righteousness and peace have kissed each other* (Psalm 85:10); and God is glorified in the highest, for peace proclaimed upon the earth.

The expression of *good-will toward men*, seems to rise upon the former. Not only peace, but acceptance and adoption in the Beloved. Sinners, who believe in the Son of God, are not merely delivered from the condemnation they have deserved, but are united to their Saviour; considered as one with him, his children, the members of his body, and made partakers of his life, and his glory. God is their portion, and heaven is their home. The Lord's satisfaction in this, as the greatest of all his works, is expressed by the prophet in such astonishing terms of condescension, as surpass our utmost conceptions: and we can only say, *Lord, what is man that you are thus mindful of him!* (Psalm 8:4). We believe, admire, and adore. *The Lord thy God in the midst of thee is mighty: he will rest in his love, he will rejoice over thee with singing* (Zephaniah 3:17).

Assuredly this song of the heavenly hosts is not the language of our hearts by nature. We once sought our pleasure and happiness in a very different way. We were indifferent to the glory of God, and strangers to his peace. And some of us are still blind to the excellencies of the gospel, and deaf to its gracious invitations. But we must not expect to sing with the great company of the redeemed hereafter, before the throne of glory, unless we learn and love their song while we are here (Revelation 15:3). They who attain to the inheritance of the saints in light, are first made meet for it in the present life, and in this way. They believe the testimony of the Scripture respecting their own guilt, unworthiness and helplessness; then they receive the record which God has given of his Son. *They renounce all confidence in the flesh* (Philippians 3:3); they rejoice in Christ Jesus, and from his fulness they derive grace to worship God in the Spirit. A sense of their obligations to the Saviour disposes them to praise him now as they can; and they rejoice in hope of seeing him ere long as he is, and that then they shall praise him as they ought. For heaven itself, as described in the Word of God, could not be a state of happiness to us, unless we are like-minded with the apostle, to *account all things loss and dung for the excellency of the knowledge of Jesus Christ our Lord* (Philippians 3:8).[1]

A hymn by John Newton, based on 2 Corinthians 13:14

May the grace of Christ our Saviour
And the Father's boundless love
With the Holy Spirit's favour
Rest upon us from above!
Thus may we abide in union
With each other, and the Lord;
And possess, in sweet communion,
Joys which earth cannot afford.[2]

---

[1] John Newton, *Messiah: Fifty Expository Discourses, on the Series of Scriptural Passages, which Form the Subject of the Celebrated Oratorio of Handel*, Vol. 1 (London: Author, 1786), 195–198.
[2] John Newton and William Cowper, *Olney Hymns* (London: T. Wilkins, 1783), 371.

Day 20

Hannah More
(1745-1833)

More was an English poet and Christian writer who was converted from the high-society life of London through the writing and ministry of John Newton. She spent the remainder of her days ministering to the poor and needy, founding Sunday schools and helping William Wilberforce abolish the slave trade.

◇◇◇◇◇◇◇◇◇◇◇◇◇◇◇◇◇◇◇◇◇◇◇◇◇◇◇◇◇

Remember Jesus Christ (2 Timothy 2:8).

In order to know how the time of Christ's birth ought to be remembered by us, I would observe that it is necessary to understand well who Christ was, and for what purpose he came on earth. It may be said in general, that it was for us men, and for our salvation, that he came down from heaven or, as the Scripture expresses it, "For the Son of Man came to seek and to save the lost... and to give his life as a ransom for many" (Luke 19:10; Mark 10:45). The world was sunk in sin, and not in sin only, but in condemnation also. Ever since the fall of our first parent Adam, man had become a sinful creature. But as in Adam all had died, so now in Christ were all (that is, all who would receive him) to be made alive. Christ, then, was the second Adam: as Adam was the *destroyer*, so Christ was the *restorer* of our race.

The devil, who is called the Prince of Darkness, had, as we are told in Scripture, become the god and the prince of this world. Christ, therefore, came into the world as a conqueror comes, to recover an empire that was lost, and to bring back the rebels to their obedience, and to happiness. He came to overthrow that kingdom of darkness which, through the power of the devil, and the corruption of man, had been set up. "The reason the Son of God appeared was to destroy the works of the devil" (1 John 3:8). He came "to redeem us from all lawlessness and to purify for himself a people for his own possession who are zealous for good works" (Titus 2:14).

But how does Christ fulfil his purpose of delivering us? First, I would observe that he lived a most holy life; hereby setting before us an example that we should tread in his steps. He went about doing good: never was any one so kind and gracious to all who came to him, as Jesus Christ. I would here observe also, that he preached the gospel to mankind; he told us what we must believe and do, in order to enter into the kingdom of heaven. Through him also, the Holy Spirit of God is granted to us. And to crown all, he died for us. He was nailed to the cross, and suffered a cruel death for our sakes, bearing the wrath of God in our stead. "In this is love, not that we have loved God but that he loved us and sent his Son to be the propitiation for our sins" (1 John 4:10). Christ is that Lamb of God who has been offered up as a sacrifice (Ephesians 5:2) and "who takes away the sin of the world!" (John 1:29).

Now then, let us rejoice, and say triumphantly, with the prophet of old, "To us a child is born, to us a son is given" (Isaiah 9:6)—"Behold, (said the angels) I bring you good news of great joy; for unto you is born this day in the city of David a Savior, who is Christ the Lord. Glory to God in the highest, and on earth peace among those with whom he is pleased!" (Luke 2:10–11). Oh! how many thousands have had reason to bless the season which we are now commemorating—the season of the birth of Jesus Christ! The world, it is true, is still wicked, for there are many who do not believe in this Saviour—and there are not a few who think they believe in him and who do not. Nevertheless, even the world in general has been the better for his coming, for the thick darkness is past, and the true light now shines.

But who can calculate the blessing which Christianity has been to thousands of true believers? How many lives have been made holy here on earth; how many hearts have been cheered and comforted by it; how many deaths, which would otherwise have been most gloomy, have been rendered joyful and triumphant; and, above all, how many immortal souls have been saved and made happy to all eternity, through faith in this blessed Redeemer? "My sheep," says Christ, "My sheep hear my voice, and I know them, and they follow me. I give them eternal life, and they will never perish, and no one will snatch them out of my hand" (John 10:27–28).

How shall I sufficiently bless God for Jesus Christ![1]

Prayer of Hannah More

Lord, pour out the grace of thy Holy Spirit on me and mine without measure; teach us to love thee with all our hearts, minds, souls and strength, and to devote the remainder of our lives to thy service, and to the glory of our Lord and Saviour Jesus Christ.[2]

---

[1] Hannah More, *A New Christmas Tract* (London: J. G. & F. Rivington, 1836), 4–10.
[2] William Roberts, *Memoirs of the Life and Correspondence of Mrs. Hannah More*, Vol. 2 (New York: Harper & Brothers, 1835), 113.

Day 21

J.C. Ryle
(1816–1900)

Ryle was an Anglican bishop in Liverpool, England. He advocated for reform within the Church of England, emphasizing biblical doctrine, expository preaching and the contemporary relevance of the church. His most famous book is *Holiness*.

"She will bear a son, and you shall call his name Jesus, for he will save his people from their sins." All this took place to fulfill what the Lord had spoken by the prophet: "Behold, the virgin shall conceive and bear a son, and they shall call his name Immanuel" (which means, God with us) (Matthew 1:21-23).

Let us observe the two names given to our Lord in these verses. One describes his *office*; the other his *nature*. Both are deeply interesting. The name *Jesus* means *Saviour*. It is given to our Lord because "he will save his people from their sins." He saves them from the *guilt* of sin, by washing them in his own atoning blood. He saves them from the *dominion* of sin, by putting in their hearts the sanctifying Spirit. He saves them from the *presence* of sin, when he takes them out of this world to rest with him. He will save them from all the *consequences* of sin, when he shall give them a glorious body at the last day. Blessed and holy are Christ's people! From sorrow, cross and conflict they are not saved. But they are saved from *sin* for evermore. They are cleansed from guilt by Christ's blood. They are made fit for heaven by Christ's Spirit. This is salvation. He who cleaves to sin is not yet saved.

Jesus is a very encouraging name to heavy-laden sinners. He who is King of kings and Lord of lords might lawfully have taken some more high-sounding title. But he does not do so. The rulers of this world have often called themselves Great, Conquerors, Bold, Magnificent, and the like. The Son of God is content to call himself *Saviour*. The souls which desire salvation may draw near to the Father with boldness, and have access with confidence through Christ. It is his office and his delight to show mercy. Happy is that person, who trusts not merely in vague notions of God's mercy and goodness, but in *Jesus*.

The other name in these verses is scarcely less interesting than that just referred to. It is the name which is given to our Lord from his nature, as "God manifest in the flesh." He is called *Immanuel*, "God with us."

Let us take care that we have clear views of our Lord Jesus Christ's nature and person. It is a point of the deepest importance. We should settle it firmly in our minds, that our Saviour is perfect Man as well as perfect God, and perfect God as well as perfect Man. If we once lose sight of this great foundation truth, we may run into fearful heresies. The name *Immanuel* takes in the whole mystery. Jesus is "God with us." He had a nature like our own in all things, sin only excepted. But though Jesus was "with us" in human flesh and blood, he was at the same time very *God*.

Would you have a strong foundation for your faith and hope? Then keep in constant view your Saviour's *divinity*. He in whose blood you are taught to trust is the *almighty* God. All power is his in heaven and earth. None can pluck you out of his hand. If you are a true believer in Jesus, let not your heart be troubled or afraid.

Would you have sweet comfort in suffering and trial? Then keep in constant view your Saviour's *humanity*. He is the Man Christ Jesus, who lay on the bosom of the virgin Mary, as a little infant, and knows the heart of a man. He can be touched with the feeling of your infirmities. He has himself experienced Satan's temptations. He has endured hunger. He has shed tears. He has felt pain. Trust him at all times with all your sorrows. He will not despise you. Pour out all your heart before him in prayer, and keep nothing back. He can sympathize with his people.

Let these thoughts sink down into our minds. Let us bless God for the encouraging truths which the first chapter of the New Testament contains. It tells us of One who "saves his people from their sins." But this is not all. It tells us that this Saviour is *Immanuel*, God himself, and yet God with us, God manifest in human flesh like our own. This is glad tidings. This is indeed good news. Let us feed on these truths in our hearts by faith with thanksgiving.[1]

Prayer of J.C. Ryle

I pray God that everyone of us may have a hope in which Christ is all; Christ the beginning, and Christ the end; the Alpha and the Omega; the first and the last; the Foundation, the Corner-stone, the strength and the stay. If it be not so, alas! for his soul. But he that builds on Jesus shall never be confounded. Now may mercy and truth, grace and peace, be with you all this year, and till the Lord comes.[2]

---

[1] J.C. Ryle, *Expository Thoughts on the Gospels: St. Matthew* (New York: Robert Carter & Brothers, 1860), 6–9.
[2] J.C. Ryle, *A Ministerial Address for the Beginning of the New Year* (Ipswich: E. Hunt, 1846), 16.

Day 22

Charles Haddon Spurgeon
(1834-1892)

Spurgeon was a Baptist pastor and theologian, called the "Prince of Preachers." A most prolific author, he left behind a legacy of over 3,500 sermons, books and numerous devotional materials. He also founded a pastor's college, an orphanage and almshouses. His preaching was Christ-centred, evangelistic in its appeal and rooted in the Scriptures.

◇◇◇◇◇◇◇◇◇◇◇◇◇◇◇◇◇◇◇◇◇◇◇◇◇◇◇

"Where is he who has been born king of the Jews?"
(Matthew 2:2)

A very singular thing is this, that Jesus Christ was said to have been "born king of the Jews." Very few have ever been "born king." Men are born princes, but they are seldom born kings. I do not think you can find an instance in history where any infant was born king. He was the prince of Wales, perhaps, and he had to wait a number of years, till his father died, and then they manufactured him into a king, by putting a crown on his head; and a sacred chrism, and other silly things; but he was not *born* a king. I remember no one who was born a king except Jesus; and there is emphatic meaning in that verse that we sing

"Born thy people to deliver;
Born a child, and yet a king."

The moment that he came on earth he was a king. He did not wait till his majority that he might take his empire; but as soon as his eye greeted the sunshine he was a king; from the moment that his little hands grasped anything, they grasped a sceptre, as soon as his pulse beat, and his blood began to flow, his heart beat royally, and his pulse beat an imperial measure and his blood flowed in a kingly current. He was born a king.

My brother, hast thou submitted to the sway of Jesus? Is he ruler in thine heart, or is he not? We may know Israel by this: Christ is come into their hearts, to be ruler over them. "Oh!" saith one, "I do as I please, I was never in bondage to any man." Ah! then thou hatest the rule of Christ. "Oh!" says another, "I submit myself to my minister, to my clergyman, or to my priest, and I think that what he tells me is enough, for he is my ruler." Dost thou? Ah! poor slave, thou knowest not thy dignity; for nobody is thy lawful ruler but the Lord Jesus Christ. "Ay," says another, "I have professed his religion, and I am his follower." But doth he rule in thine heart? Doth he command thy will? Doth he guide thy judgement? Dost thou ever seek counsel at his hand in thy difficulties? Art thou desirous to honour him, and to put crowns upon his head? Is he thy ruler? If so, then thou art one of Israel; for it is written, "He shall come to be ruler in Israel."

Blessed Lord Jesus! Thou art ruler in thy people's hearts, and thou ever shalt be; we want no other ruler save thyself, and we will submit to none other. We are free, because we are the servants of Christ; we are at liberty, because he is our ruler, and we know no bondage and no slavery, because Jesus Christ alone is monarch of our hearts. He came "to be ruler in Israel;" and mark you, that mission of his is not quite fulfilled yet, and shall not be till the latter-day glories. In a little while you shall see Christ come again, to be ruler over his people Israel, and ruler over them not only as *spiritual* Israel, but even as natural Israel, for the Jews shall be restored to their land, and the tribes of Jacob shall yet sing in the halls of their temple; unto God there shall yet again be offered Hebrew songs of praise, and the heart of the unbelieving

Jew shall be melted at the feet of the true Messiah. In a short time, he who at his birth was hailed King of the Jews by Easterns, and at his death was written King of the Jews by a Western, shall be called King of the Jews everywhere—yes, King of the Jews and Gentiles also—in that universal monarchy whose dominion shall be co-extensive with the habitable globe, and whose duration shall be coeval [having the same age] with time itself. He came to be a ruler in Israel, and a ruler most decidedly he shall be, when he shall reign among his people with his ancients gloriously.

Prayer of Charles Haddon Spurgeon

Sweet Lord Jesus! Thou whose goings forth were of old, even from everlasting, thou hast not left thy goings forth yet. Oh! that thou wouldst go forth this day, to cheer the faint, to help the weary, to bind up our wounds, to comfort our distresses! Go forth, we beseech thee, to conquer sinners, to subdue hard hearts, to break the iron gates of sinners' lusts and cut the iron bars of their sins in pieces! O Jesus! go forth; and when thou goest forth, come thou to me![1]

---

[1] Charles Spurgeon, *The New Park Street Pulpit*, Vol. 2 (London: Passmore and Alabaster, 1856), 29–32.

Day 23

Dwight L. Moody
(1837-1899)

Moody was a pastor and evangelist who founded Moody Church, Moody Bible Institute and Moody Publishers in Chicago, Illinois. He also helped pioneer the Sunday School movement in America.

And the angel said to them, "Fear not, for behold, I bring you good news of great joy that will be for all the people. For unto you is born this day in the city of David a Savior, who is Christ the Lord" (Luke 2:10-11).

I believe no better news ever came out of heaven than the gospel of Jesus Christ. I believe no better news has ever fallen upon the ears of men than the gospel of Jesus Christ. No news like this—and there never will be any news like it—a Saviour is born unto you. And now I want to tell you why the gospel is good news—that is, why it is good news to me. It has taken out of my path the very bitterest enemies I have ever had. *Death* is a bitter enemy to the human race; and while we are gathered in this meeting today, it may steal into our dwellings and take away the dearest friend we have got on earth. It may take the wife of your bosom; it may take the children that are now full of glee and full of joy at the anticipation of Christmas coming; and you may go home and find that death has entered into your dwelling and thrown a dark shadow across your path, and thrown a blight across your threshold. Death is an enemy, but the gospel of Jesus Christ tells me that that very enemy has been conquered. When Christ came into the world, he met death, and he conquered him. But then if we are in Christ, we have got the victory. Death has had his hand on Christ once; he will never have his hand on him again. "I am he that shall live. Behold, I live forevermore." He lives; and if I have Christ, death cannot touch that new life. "He that hath the Son hath life." If I have Christ formed in me, the hope of glory, death cannot touch that. We have a new life, and that is the good news.

Well, then, the other enemy is *sin*. I used to think it would be an awful time when a man had to render an account of his sins; but do you know the gospel tells me that if I believe on the Lord Jesus Christ, that out of love to me he has just taken all my sins and cast them behind his back—behind God's back. If God has put them away; if God has washed them away, they are clean gone; if God has buried our sins, they are buried so deep that they will never have a resurrection. No fiend of hell, no devil can find our sins when God buries them. When God forgives a man, when God justifies a man, he is justified; if God puts away our sins, they are put away forever; that is what the gospel tells me. Isn't that good news? Isn't it good news to be told you have had your sins put away; that you have had them blotted out for time and eternity? God says, "I will blot them out as a thick cloud." Well, that enemy is gone. Sin is out of the way, and what an enemy it is. How it has cursed this earth; how it has broken up families; how it has ruined households. But God came down to the earth, and he says, "I forgive you, if you will believe on my Son; if you will take him."

Well, the next enemy is *judgement*. And I used to think it would be a terrible hour when we would stand before God and have all the sins that we had committed from childhood up all blazoned out before the assembled universe; sins that we had committed in secret; sins that we committed in childhood—all of them. But do you know that blessed gospel tells me that Jesus Christ went into judgement for me, and I haven't got to go there for sin? Christ was judged for us. "He was wounded for our transgressions; he was bruised for our iniquities; and the chastisement of our peace was laid upon him; with his stripes we are healed, and in his own self he bore our sins in his own body on the tree." Jesus Christ has paid the debt. He took my place when he died on Calvary. He was the sinner's substitute; he died in our stead; he that knew no sin became sin for us, and upon the sacrifice of himself has put away our sins. Now you see, we are not going to come to judgement for sin; that is passed; that is behind me; death, grave, sin and judgement are all behind me.

As I got up this morning the first thought that came to my mind was, "God, I thank thee for sending Christ into this world." How it has lit up my little home. How my children are filled with joy that Christ came. And the best thing you can do today is to receive Christ and then thank God for sending him; and then there will be light, peace and joy; all of these blessings will come right into your heart.

Prayer of Dwight L. Moody

Our heavenly Father, we pray that these dear friends today may be wise; that they may take the gift of God, which is eternal life; that they may go down to their homes justified; that they may have these great enemies that stand in every man's path, overcome by the Man of Sorrows; that they may take him that came into the world and gave his life for the world—that they may take him to be their way, their truth, and their life; that they may this day and this hour believe on the Lord Jesus Christ and be saved. Let thy blessing, we pray thee, rest upon the homes throughout this great city, and as the children shall gather on their festive occasion around the Christmas tree and in the family homes, may the blessing of God come upon them, and may there be a great multitude in this city that shall receive this coming season God's Christmas gift. And thy name shall have the praise and the glory. Amen.[1]

---

[1] Dwight L. Moody, *The New Sermons of Dwight Lyman Moody* (New York: Goodspeed, 1880), 777–785.

Day 24

G. Campbell Morgan
(1863-1945)

Morgan was pastor of Westminster Chapel in London, England, and a professor at Biola University in Los Angeles. He was known as an expository preacher who defended the authority and inerrancy of the Scriptures.

From of old no one has heard or perceived by the ear, no eye has seen a God besides you, who acts for those who wait for him (Isaiah 64:4).

The whole teaching of Holy Scripture places the *incarnation* at the centre of the methods of God with a sinning race. Toward that incarnation everything moved until its accomplishment, finding therein fulfilment and explanation. The messages of the prophets and seers and the songs of the psalmists trembled with more or less certainty toward the final music which announced the coming of Christ. The Gospel stories are all concerned with the coming of Christ, with his mission and his message. The letters of the New Testament have all to do with the fact of the incarnation, and its correlated doctrines and duties. The last book of the Bible is a book, the true title of which is *The Unveiling of the Christ*. It is surely important, therefore, that we should understand its purposes in the economy of God. There is a fourfold statement of purpose declared in the New Testament: the purpose to reveal the Father; the purpose to put away sin; the purpose to destroy the works of the devil; and the purpose to establish by another advent the kingdom of God in the world. Christ was in conflict with all that was contrary to the purposes of God in individual, social, national and racial life. There is a sense in which when we have said this we have stated the whole meaning of his coming. His revelation of the Father was toward this end; his putting away of sin was part of this very process; and his second advent will be for the complete and final overthrow of all the works of the devil. Nineteen centuries ago the Son of God was manifested, and during those centuries in the lives of hundreds, thousands, he has destroyed the works of the devil, mastered death by the gift of life; cast darkness out by the incoming light; turned the selfishness of avarice and jealousy into love, joy, peace, longsuffering, kindness, goodness. He has taken hold of lawless men and made them into the willing, glad bond-servants of God. So he has destroyed the works of the devil.

The incarnation was the invasion of human history by One who snatched the sceptre from the usurper. It was the intrusion of forces into human history which dissolved the consistency of the works of the devil and caused them to break and fail. "How long, O Lord, how long?" is the cry of the heart of the saint today. Yet let us take heart as we look back and know that the victorious force has operated for nineteen centuries, and always toward consummation. Still, the works of the devil are manifest; the works of the flesh are manifest. Yes, but the fruit of the Spirit of life, which has come through the advent of Christ, is also manifest. All over the world today on many a branch of the vine of the Father's planting, the rich clusters of fruit are to be found. All, so far, is but preliminary. It is twilight only. High noon has not arrived; but it is twilight, and the noon must come.

We are all conscious that nothing is perfect; that the things which Christ came to do are not yet done; that the works of the devil are not yet finally destroyed; that sins are not yet experimentally taken away; that in the spiritual consciousness of the race, God is not yet perfectly known. "Now we see not yet all things subjected to him." The victory does not seem to be won. It is impossible to read the story of the incarnation, and to believe in it, and to follow the history of the centuries that have followed upon that incarnation, without feeling in one's deepest heart that something more is needed, that the incarnation was preparatory, and that the consummation of its meaning can only be brought about by another coming, as personal, as definite, as positive, as real in human history as was the first.

Every New Testament writer presents this truth as part of the common Christian faith. Belief in the *personal actual second advent of Jesus* gave the bloom to primitive Christianity, and constituted the power of the early Christians to laugh in the face of death, and to overcome all forces that were against them. There is nothing more necessary in our day than a new declaration of this vital fact of Christian faith.[1]

Prayer of G. Campbell Morgan

O Jesus, by thy infinite compassion, by thy love passing all human telling, thou hast conquered me. I am come to thee. Take my life, poor, weak, insufficient by every standard of human measurement, but let thy life flow into it, through it, that my life may make some little contribution to the realization of thy great purpose. I yield to thee all I am, and have, and hope for, in order that through me some part of thy kingdom may come and thy will be done. Amen.[2]

---

[1] G. Campbell Morgan, *The Fundamentals*, Vol. 1 (Chicago: Testimony Publishing Company, 1909), 29–50.
[2] *Prayers We Love to Pray*, ed. Edward Pell (Richmond, VA: Robert Harding Company, 1909), 37.

Day 25

D. Martyn Lloyd-Jones
(1899-1981)

Lloyd-Jones was a pastor in Wales and later at Westminster Chapel in London. He was known for his expository and doctrinal preaching. He was also influential within Inter-Varsity Fellowship and his support of Banner of Truth publishing and the Puritan Conference.

"He has filled the hungry with good things, and the rich he has sent away empty" (Luke 1:53).

The most surprising thing that has ever happened in this world is the coming of the Son of God into it. The most revolutionary thing in the world today is the gospel. Why? Because it is the exact opposite almost of anything that you and I would ever have imagined or thought of. Look at the way in which God has done this thing. When God comes to take the action that is to save mankind, how does he do it? Who would ever have anticipated or imagined that he would do it by the birth of a helpless babe? We wouldn't start by doing it through a babe. We'd have somebody suddenly coming out of him. Great apparition. Great display. We are fond of drama. We are fond of propaganda. We are fond of doing things in a big way, of blowing trumpets and a great announcement. That's our way. It wasn't God's way. But come, let us look at it more in detail. Notice the way in which God's action for the salvation of men condemns and indeed demolishes. "The rich," we are told, "he has sent away empty." This is not to be taken in a material sense primarily, but in a moral sense. What is the effect of the coming of the Son of God into this world? It is to send the rich away empty. This was the whole trouble with the Pharisees and that is why they hated our Lord. That is why they finally conspired to crucify and to kill him. The effect of the coming of the Son of God upon the Pharisees was to send them away empty. And they were so rich! But when they listened to the preaching of the Son of God, they could see their righteousness disappearing; all they had boasted of, all they had gloated in, all they had prided themselves on: their exceptional righteousness, they who had never committed adultery. "Wait a minute," says the Son of God; "have you ever looked on a woman to lust? If you have, you have committed adultery with her, in your heart. That is what matters." And their righteousness had gone. They were all guilty. They thought they were innocent. They were not! He took them through point by point in the Sermon on the Mount. He showed them the spiritual character of God's law. And these men, who thought they had kept the law of God to perfection, found themselves guilty on every point. And they hated him. Why? He sent them away empty. They thought they were rich.

That is what he has always done. Men and women are very satisfied with themselves and their own lives until they look into the face of Jesus Christ. But the moment they look at him and listen to his interpretation of God's law, they begin to say, that "There is none righteous, no, not one" (Romans 3:10). A man says: "I'm a good fellow, I've got my code, I'm better than this man, I am much better than that one, I do a lot of good, I'm wonderful"—as the Pharisee said it in the temple (Luke 18:11). And then he finds that God's law is that, "You shall love the Lord your God with all your heart and with all your soul and with all your strength and with all your mind, and your neighbor as yourself" (Luke 10:27). And he has not started, he is nowhere. He listens to Christ saying: "Blessed are the poor in spirit"

(Matthew 5:3), and he is so full of pride, he is damned already. He goes away empty. "Blessed are the meek" (Matthew 5:5), and he is the opposite to meekness. "Blessed are those who hunger and thirst for righteousness, for they shall be satisfied" (Matthew 5:6), and he is boasting of his righteousness. He's sent empty away.

What a phrase is this: "He has filled the hungry with good things." "Blessed are those who hunger and thirst for righteousness." Why? Oh, they shall be filled! "The rich he has sent away empty." We have seen that. But look at the opposite: the hungry, the man who feels he is a sinner, vile. The man who feels he is a cad; the man who cannot understand himself. The man who feels he is rotten. The man who says to himself, "In me, that is, in my flesh, dwells no good thing" (Romans 7:18). The man who says: "Wretched man that I am! Who will deliver me from this body of death?" (Romans 7:24). The man who says: "Everything I do is wrong; it's tarnished, it's sinful; my best actions are ignoble. There is nothing right about me at all. I hate myself. I cannot deliver myself. What can be done with such a wretch as I am?" What about him? He shall be "filled with good things." What are they? Well, righteousness: he is hungering and thirsting after righteousness. He is poor in spirit, he is mourning because of his sinfulness and the sins he has committed. He does not know what to do. Blessed is such a man, says Christ. He shall be filled with righteousness. It means that God sent his Son into this world in order that we might be made righteous. We cannot make ourselves righteous. The whole world has failed. Men and women in their blind manner try to seek it in a sense, but they cannot. They are wrong in their very notions. But suddenly they are awakened and convicted; they want it. Suddenly, they are given it. It is all in Christ.

Now this sounds incredible. That is why people do not believe it. But this is the gospel. What does the gospel tell me? It tells me that if I believe in the Lord Jesus Christ truly and trust myself to him, then his righteousness is upon me; my sins are blotted out as if I had never committed a single sin in my life. God pronounces me to be righteous. He has put to my account the righteousness of Christ. I am a pauper; my books are empty; I am damned; I am doomed. Suddenly, the wealth of the Son of God is put into my account. "He has filled the hungry with good things!"[1]

Prayer of D. Martyn Lloyd-Jones

We thank thee, O God, we realize what we are apart from thy grace. And to see in a new and in a wondrous manner the exceeding riches of thy grace and the endlessness of the ocean of thy love to us. O God, we thank thee for everything that thou hast enabled us to see of the truth concerning thyself in Christ Jesus. We thank thee, O God, for a larger and a deeper apprehension of this wondrous plan of redemption and of salvation. We thank thee, O God, for bringing us to see more and more, that it is something which is eternal, something that was worked out, and elaborated even before the very foundation of the world itself, something which goes on until sin and evil shall finally be destroyed and everything in heaven, and earth, and under the earth shall acknowledge the lordship and the name of thy dear Son. Amen.[2]

---

[1] D. Martyn Lloyd-Jones, "The Magnificat 3" accessed April 5, 2024, www.mljtrust.org/sermons/other-sermons/the-magnificat-3.

[2] www.mljtrust.org/sermons/prayer/congregational-prayers-martyn-lloyd-jones.

Day 26

Dietrich Bonhoeffer
(1906-1945)

Bonhoeffer was a German Lutheran pastor who was imprisoned and martyred by the Nazi regime. He helped found the Confessing Church, and is known for his books *The Cost of Discipleship* and *Life Together*.

His name shall be called Wonderful Counselor, Mighty God, Everlasting Father, Prince of Peace! (Isaiah 9:6)

Who is this child, of whom the prophets speak and at whose birth heaven and earth rejoice? It is only with stammering tongues that we can speak his name or seek to describe what is embraced by this name. Words limp and stumble when they attempt to say who this child is. Yes, when human lips try to express the name of this child, strange word-pictures emerge, which we do not know: "Wonderful Counselor," "Mighty God," "Everlasting Father," "Prince of Peace." Every title in these words comes from unfathomable depths and taken together they try to encompass one single name: *Jesus*.

This child is called, "Wonderful Counselor." In him, the wonder of all wonders has taken place. The birth of the Saviour-child comes out of the eternal counsel of God. God gave us his Son in the form of a human child. God became Man, the Word became flesh. That is the wonder of God's love for us, and it is the unfathomable counsel of God which wins and delivers us. And because this child of God is uniquely *Wonderful Counselor*, he is therefore himself also the source of all wonder and all counsel. Anyone who recognizes Jesus as the Son of God, whose every word and every deed is a wonder, will find in him the profoundest and most helpful counsel in all times of trouble and questioning. Yes, before his lips can speak, he is full of wonder and full of counsel. Go to the child in the manger and you will find in him wonder upon wonder, counsel upon counsel.

This child is called "Mighty God." The child in the manger is none other than God himself. Nothing greater could be said: God becomes a child. In the Jesus-child of Mary dwells almighty God. Just take that in for a moment! Don't speak, don't think any further! Stand quietly and wait before this statement, that God has become a child! Here, he is poor like us, wretched like us, and helpless like us, a child of flesh and blood like us, our brother. And yet he is *God*, almighty God. Where is the divinity, where is the power of this child? It is in the divine love by which he becomes like us. His pitiable condition in the manger is his power. In the power of love, he overcomes the chasm between God and man, powerfully overcoming sin and death, he forgives sin and raises from the dead. Kneel low before this pitiable manger, before this child of poor people and speak in faith with stammering tongue, the words of the prophets, "Almighty God," and he will be your God and your power.

"Everlasting Father"—how can this be the name of the child? Only if the everlasting fatherly love of God is revealed in this child and that this child will do nothing other than bring the love of the Father to the earth. In this way, the Father and the Son are One, and he who sees the Son, sees the Father. This child will do nothing of himself, he is not a wonder child in the human sense, but an obedient child of his heavenly Father. At the time of his birth, he brought eternity to earth. As Son of God, he brings to us all the love of the heavenly Father. Go then to the manger, to seek and find the everlasting Father, who has now become also your loving Father.

"Prince of Peace"—where God comes to people in love to join with them, peace is established between God and humankind, and also among ourselves, person to person. If you are afraid of the wrath of God, go to the child in the manger and let him give you the peace of God. If you are in strife and hatred with your neighbour, come and see how God, out of his great love, has dealt with your neighbour and will reconcile you both. In the world, power rules. This child is the Prince of Peace. Where he is, peace rules!

"Wonderful Counselor," "Mighty God," "Everlasting Father," "Prince of Peace." This is what we say at the manger in Bethlehem. Our words are confirmed by a glance at the divine child. We try to grasp in phrases what is contained for us in this name: *Jesus*.

Prayer of Dietrich Bonhoeffer

God, we wait for your salvation, your judgement, your love and your peace. Jesus speak to us again, "Behold I stand at the door and knock." Help us now to say, "Yes, come Lord Jesus." Amen."[1]

---

[1] *Dietrich Bonhoeffer's Christmas Sermons*, ed. Edwin Robertson (Grand Rapids, MI: Zondervan, 1954), 153–155, 56.

Day 27

J.I. Packer
(1926–2020)

Packer was an Anglican pastor in England and later a professor at Regent College in Vancouver, Canada. He served as general editor of the English Standard Version translation, and wrote numerous books including *Knowing God*.

The first man was from the earth, a man of dust; the second man is from heaven (1 Corinthians 15:47).

It is no wonder that thoughtful people find the gospel of Jesus Christ hard to believe, for the realities with which it deals pass man's understanding. But it is sad that so many make faith harder than it need be, by finding difficulties in the wrong places. Take the atonement, for instance. Many feel difficulty there. How, they ask, can we believe that the death of Jesus of Nazareth—one man, expiring on a Roman gibbet—put away a world's sins? How can that death have any bearing on God's forgiveness of our sins today? Or take the resurrection, which seems to many a stumbling-block. How, they ask, can we believe Jesus rose physically from the dead? Granted, it is hard to deny the tomb was empty—but surely the difficulty of believing Jesus emerged from it into unending bodily life is even greater? Is not any form of the theory of temporary resuscitation after a faint, or of the stealing of the body, easier to credit than the Christian doctrine of the resurrection? Or, again, take the virgin birth, which has been widely denied among Protestants in this century. How, people ask, can one possibly believe in such a biological anomaly? Or take the gospel miracles; many find a source of difficulty here. Granted, they say, Jesus healed (it is hard, on the evidence, to doubt that he did, and in any case history has known other healers); how can one believe he walked on the water, or fed the 5,000, or raised the dead? Stories like that are surely quite incredible. With these and similar problems many minds on the fringes of faith are deeply perplexed today.

But in fact the real difficulty, because the supreme mystery with which the gospel confronts us, does not lie here at all. It lies, not in the Good Friday message of atonement, nor in the Easter message of resurrection, but in the Christmas message of *incarnation*. The really staggering Christian claim is that Jesus of Nazareth was God made man—that the second Person of the Godhead became the "second man" (1 Corinthians 15:47), determining human destiny, the second representative Head of the race, and that he took humanity without loss of deity, so that Jesus of Nazareth was as truly and fully divine as he was human. Here are two mysteries for the price of one—the plurality of Persons within the unity of God, and the union of Godhead and manhood in the Person of Jesus. It is here, in the thing that happened at the first Christmas, that the profoundest and most unfathomable depths of the Christian revelation lie. "The Word was made flesh" (John 1:14); God became man; the divine Son became a Jew; the Almighty appeared on earth as a helpless human baby, unable to do more than lie and stare and wriggle and make noises, needing to be fed and changed and taught to talk like any other child. And there was no illusion or deception in this: the babyhood of the Son of God was a reality. The more you think about it, the more staggering it gets. Nothing in fiction is so fantastic as is this truth of the incarnation.

If Jesus had been no more than a very remarkable, godly man, the difficulties in believing what the New Testament tells us about his life and work would be truly mountainous. But if Jesus was the same Person as the eternal Word, the Father's agent in creation, "through whom also he created the world" (Hebrews 1:2), it is no wonder if fresh acts of creative power marked his coming into this world, and his life in it, and his exit from it. It is not strange that he, the author of life, should rise from the dead. If he was truly God the Son, it is much more startling that he should die than that he should rise again. And if the immortal Son of God did really submit to taste death, it is not strange that such a death should have saving significance for a doomed race. Once we grant that Jesus was divine, it becomes unreasonable to find difficulty in any of this; it is all of a piece, and hangs together completely. The incarnation is in itself an unfathomable mystery, but it makes sense of everything else the New Testament contains.[1]

Prayer of J.I. Packer

Our gracious God, our hearts are thrilled, our hearts overflow with joy as we contemplate the riches of thy grace. We thank thee for what we have tasted of assurance that these things include us, that we have an interest in thy saving mercy, that we are children of God. O, increase this blessed witness of the Spirit in us more and more. So bless these meditations to us we beseech thee. In Jesus name, Amen.[2]

---

[1] J.I. Packer, *Knowing God* (Downers Grove, IL: InterVarsity Press, 1973), 45–47.
[2] J.I. Packer, "Sanctification and Assurance"; accessed April 12, 2024; www.sermonaudio.com/sermon/2190483054.

Day 28

James Montgomery Boice
(1938–2000)

> Boice was a theologian and pastor of Tenth Presbyterian Church in Philadelphia. His writings included expositional commentaries, doctrinal and practical theology books, particularly his *Foundations of the Christian Faith* and a collection of hymns.

∞∞∞∞∞∞∞∞∞∞∞∞∞∞∞∞∞∞∞∞

And the angel said to them, "Fear not, for behold, I bring you good news of great joy that will be for all the people" (Luke 2:10).

There are many emotions associated with observing Christmas, but there is no emotion so characteristic of Christmas as *joy*. The whole atmosphere of Christmas is joyful, and it has been so ever since the angels announced the birth of Jesus to the shepherds in the fields. That is why we sing about joy so often in our carols:

O come, all ye faithful, Joyful and triumphant…
Dear desire of every nation, Joy of every longing heart…
Joyful, all ye nations rise, Join the triumph of the skies…

And best of all…

Joy to the world! The Lord is come…

We find joy throughout the Christmas story, in the experience of the story's main characters. The best-known statement of joy is the utterance of the angels to the shepherds. But those who announced joy to the shepherds had themselves first experienced it, which was why they were singing praises to God in the night skies above Bethlehem. And why should they not have been singing? The Lord Jesus Christ later told us that the angels rejoice in heaven over even one sinner who repents (Luke 15:7, 10). So how could they not rejoice over the birth of him who was to save not only a solitary sinner, but many? The rejoicing of the angels tells us there was heavenly joy at the birth of Jesus.

The shepherds also rejoiced. If the rejoicing of the angels was a heavenly joy, theirs was clearly an earthly and very humble joy. They might have missed this joy in a variety of ways, thinking perhaps that the angels' "good news" was for others more important or better instructed than themselves, a mistake many people make today. But they did not make this mistake. They hurried to Bethlehem, saw the baby, and then returned to their sheep. "And the shepherds returned, glorifying and praising God for all they had heard and seen, as it had been told them" (Luke 2:20). If the Saviour had been born in a palace, these men would have been turned away at the door. Jesus had been born where any person could come to him. That is still true today, and it is still a reason for joy. Jesus is accessible.

The shepherds were filled with joy, but I am sure this did not hinder them from noticing the joy of Jesus' mother, Mary. The Bible says that in her joy Mary "treasured up all these things, pondering them in her heart" (Luke 2:19). What about Joseph? Joseph must have been overcome with joy too. His would have been an awesome joy, for an angel had appeared to him months before to explain Mary's conception as something unique and supernatural: "Joseph, son of David, do not fear to take Mary as your wife, for that which is conceived in her is from the Holy Spirit. She will bear a son, and you shall call his name Jesus, for he will save his people from their sins" (Matthew 1:20–21).

The last people to come upon the scene are the wise men. The wise men went to Bethlehem and, led by the star they had been following earlier, found Jesus. The text says, "When they saw the star, they rejoiced exceedingly with great joy" and that when they found the young child they "worshipped him… they offered him gifts, gold and frankincense and myrrh (Matthew 2:10–11). This was the world's Saviour—*their* Saviour. So they expressed their joy accordingly.

This brings me to the next important observation on our text, the most important thing of all from our perspective. The text says, "Fear not, for behold, I bring you good news of great joy that will be for all the people." It is for *you*, if you will come to Jesus.[1]

Prayer of James Montgomery Boice

Our Father, we talk about the joy of Christmas. By your grace grant us that greatest joy of all, as those who have been dead in their sins are made alive in Christ, who have been in the kingdom of darkness, but now by your grace are brought into his marvelous light. We pray in Jesus' name, Amen.[2]

---

[1] James Montgomery Boice, *The King has Come* (Fearn, Scotland: Christian Focus, 1992), 130–135.
[2] James Montgomery Boice, "A Mighty Ruler from a Little Town"; accessed April 11, 2024; https://thebiblestudyhour.podbean.com/e/a-mighty-ruler-from-a-little-town.

Discover other titles from Heritage Seminary Press

Confessions of an Ex-Pentecostal
By Philip D. Stairs

Philip Stairs was born and raised in a United Pentecostal (UPC) pastors' home in New Brunswick, Canada. Early on, it became clear that Phil would follow in the footsteps of his parents, Wynn and Margaret. As Phil grew in his faith, he became increasingly uncomfortable with Pentecostal-style worship and the practice of speaking in tongues as evidence of the baptism of the Holy Spirit.

By 1963, he was asking himself whether he was really a Pentecostal. Here, Phil outlines his journey out of the UPC and into ministry as a Baptist pastor. His love for his Pentecostal friends is evident, as he explains his doctrinal struggles and how and why he left the denomination. His critique of the movement is both pointed and gentle.

This is a story of courage and change, how to leave a church or denomination and how to live with integrity as a pastor. It is hoped this will encourage many believers as they navigate difficult doctrinal challenges.

ISBN 978-1-77484-180-8 (Pbk)
ISBN 978-1-77484-181-5 (eBook)
168 pages; 5.5 x 8.5"
Published October 2025

HERITAGE SEMINARY PRESS

An imprint of H&E Publishing
heritageseminarypress.com

Discover other titles from Heritage Seminary Press

The Way and the Water: Exploring Baptistic Roots
By Henk Bakker

In *The Way and the Water*, Dr. Bakker examines the history of the Baptist and Anabaptist movements, intertwined as they were in their formation, and as they arose out of persecution and the fight for religious freedom in Europe and beyond. In their struggle against state-enforced orthodoxy, they challenged the superstitions of medieval Christianity and sought to showcase the true nature of salvation and its outworking in the lives of believers, first in believer's baptism, and then in radically reoriented lives—with the way of Christ at its centre. For this, many of them suffered greatly.

It is hoped this title will encourage Baptist and Anabaptist communities to learn more about their history and consider how they can learn from each other's traditions. May it challenge us to live for Christ with greater commitment, engagement and endurance in society today.

Translated by Aize Smit

ISBN 978-1-77484-171-6 (Pbk)
ISBN 978-1-77484-172-3 (eBook)
312 pages; 5.5 x 8.5"
Published September 2025

An imprint of H&E Publishing
heritageseminarypress.com

Discover other titles from Heritage Seminary Press

A Theologian in Service of the Church: The Collected Writings of Stanley K. Fowler
Edited by Michael A.G. Haykin & Jonathan N. Cleland
Volume 1 & Volume 2

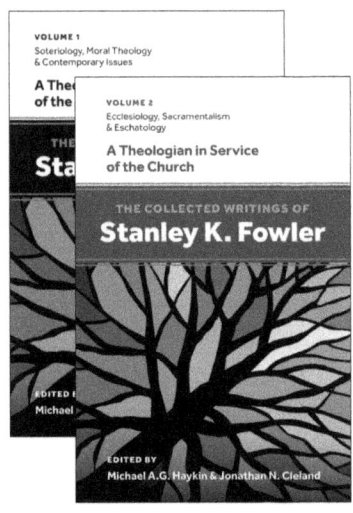

For over fifty years, the writings of Stanley K. Fowler, long-time professor of theological studies at Central Baptist Seminary, Toronto, Ont., and then Heritage College & Seminary, Cambridge, Ont., have informed and clarified theological issues for Baptists in Ontario, Canada and beyond.

Using careful biblical exegesis to address issues facing the church—such as baptism, local church autonomy, public ethics, divine sovereignty and human freedom and divorce and remarriage—Dr. Fowler has sought to equip Christians to serve the Lord well.

In this two-volume collection of his works, the editors hope the church can continue to learn from his insightful handling of the Word of God and enter deeper into relationship with the Word made flesh, Jesus Christ.

Volume 1
ISBN 978-1-77484-160-0 (Hdcvr)
ISBN 978-1-77484-157-0 (Pbk)
ISBN 978-1-77484-158-7 (Ebook)
276 pages; 5.5 x 8.5"
Published January 2025

Volume 2
ISBN 978-1-77484-163-1 (Hdcvr)
ISBN 978-1-77484-161-7 (Pbk)
ISBN 978-1-77484-162-4 (Ebook)
296 pages; 5.5 x 8.5"
Published May 2025

An imprint of H&E Publishing
heritageseminarypress.com

Discover other titles from Heritage Seminary Press

A "phoenix of women" Puritan spirituality in the letters of Brilliana Harley

Introduced and edited by Michael A.G. Azad Haykin

The life of Lady Brilliana Harley was marked by a deep and living relationship with God. A Puritan Presbyterian by conviction, Brilliana was shunned by her neighbours during the tumultuous English Civil Wars and is remembered as valiantly resisting the siege of her home by the forces of Charles I.

Brilliana's letters reveal the heart of her spirituality. While concerned about her son Edward (Ned)'s studies at Oxford, his diet and exercise, she especially encourages him about the value of a vital relationship with God. Her letters also expose the breadth of her reading and her theological acumen. As the troubles around her increased, she took increasing solace in the truths of election, the sufficiency of Christ's work and the sovereignty of God. The soil of her heart was truly warmed by "the sweet waters of God's Word."

ISBN 978-1-77484-152-5 (Pbk)
ISBN 978-1-77484-153-2 (Ebook)
172 pages; 5.5 x 8.5"
Heritage Classics
Published September 2024

HERITAGE SEMINARY PRESS

An imprint of H&E Publishing
heritageseminarypress.com

Discover other titles from Heritage Seminary Press

The oversight of souls: Essays on pastoral ministry
By Ray Van Neste

How do you understand pastoral ministry? What is the centre of your calling as a pastor? Is it difficult for your people to speak directly with you? Do you know your sheep? Do they know you?

In this book, Ray Van Neste looks to God's Word and church history to show that the oversight of souls is to be the very *heart* of pastoral ministry. The author of Hebrews writes that congregants are to: "Obey your leaders and submit to them, for they are keeping watch over your souls, as those who will have to give an account" (Hebrews 13:17). This guarding, shepherding and watching over souls requires knowledge of and meaningful engagement with the sheep and seeing them as "very dear to us" (1 Thessalonians 2:8), with the goal to "present everyone mature in Christ" (Colossians 1:28).

ISBN 978-1-77484-154-9 (Pbk)
ISBN 978-1-77484-155-6 (Ebook)
130 pages; 5.5 x 8.5"
Published October 2024

An imprint of H&E Publishing
heritageseminarypress.com

Discover other titles from Heritage Seminary Press

Losing Your Luggage: Finding Freedom from Sinful Baggage
By Rick Reed

Losing Your Luggage takes you on a journey through Romans 6–8, helping you find freedom from the sinful baggage that weighs you down. Your guide for this trip is Rick Reed, who brings out practical, down-to-earth wisdom from Paul's letter as he walks alongside you on this journey. He is one who speaks from experience and is a helpful guide to show you the main sights and lessons of these important chapters. Journey toward greater joy and freedom in Christ—and lose some sinful baggage along the route!

ISBN 978-1-77484-120-4 (Pbk)
ISBN 978-1-77484-121-1 (Ebook)
104 pages; 6 x 9"
Published June 2023

An imprint of H&E Publishing
heritageseminarypress.com

Discover other titles from Heritage Seminary Press

Life is Worship: A *festschrift* in honour of Douglas A. Thomson
Editors: David G. Barker & Michael A.G. Haykin

These essays honour the life and ministry of Dr. Doug Thomson who, as a teacher, pastor, colleague and music leader, has influenced countless lives and congregations in Ontario, Canada, and beyond. The subjects of these chapters cover themes that are precious in the life of the church—revealing how all of life is worship.

Topics include expositions of psalms and hymns, the theology of worship, spirituals, hallmarks of a worship leader, friendship in the composition of hymns, lament, etc.—even some sermons for Easter weekend. It is hoped that these essays will encourage discussion, promote the development of an understanding of the theology around worship, challenge readers to think deeply about this crucial area and, most of all, bring glory and praise to our great God.

ISBN 978-1-77484-128-0 (Pbk)
ISBN 978-1-77484-129-7 (Ebook)
364 pages; 6 x 9"
Published September 2023

An imprint of H&E Publishing
heritageseminarypress.com

Discover other titles from Heritage Seminary Press

Paul and His Christian Mission
By Michael Azad A.G. Haykin
Includes Study Guide

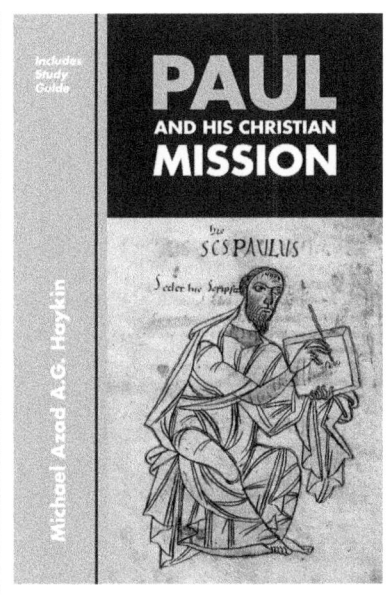

The mission of the apostle Paul is central to the New Testament, where it was vital in the establishment of the early church and spreading the gospel throughout the world of his day. This study provides a concise but rich view of Paul the man and Paul the missionary. At his conversion to Christ, Paul was given a clear mandate to bring the gospel to the Gentiles. Paul loved the church, and he was zealous to win the lost to Christ. He appreciated and cultivated co-labourers in the work of the gospel, as he depended on the power of the Holy Spirit.

Paul's experience challenges the reader. Study guide questions are provided to help reflect on and apply the things that are learned in this short, focused study of Paul's life.

ISBN 978-1-77484-106-8 (Pbk)
ISBN 978-1-77484-107-5 (Ebook)
88 pages; 5.5 x 8.5"
Published December 2022

An imprint of H&E Publishing
heritageseminarypress.com

Dominus Deus fortitudo mea | The sovereign Lord is my strength

www.ingramcontent.com/pod-product-compliance
Lightning Source LLC
Chambersburg PA
CBHW061209070526
44583CB00025B/3177